Can God Come Out To Play?

Can God Come Out To Play?

Liturgy Ceremony Ritual

SALLY ARMOUR WOTTON

RESOURCE *Publications* • Eugene, Oregon

CAN GOD COME OUT TO PLAY?
Liturgy Ceremony Ritual

Copyright © 2016 Sally Armour Wotton. All rights reserved. Except for brief quotations in critical publications or reviews, no part of this book may be reproduced in any manner without prior written permission from the publisher. Write: Permissions, Wipf and Stock Publishers, 199 W. 8th Ave., Suite 3, Eugene, OR 97401.

Resource Publications
An Imprint of Wipf and Stock Publishers
199 W. 8th Ave., Suite 3
Eugene, OR 97401

www.wipfandstock.com

PAPERBACK ISBN: 978-1-4982-3798-7
HARDCOVER ISBN: 978-1-4982-3800-7
EBOOK ISBN: 978-1-4982-3799-4

Manufactured in the U.S.A.   06/20/16

This book is lovingly dedicated to my liturgical playmates, Kelly Walker and Alexandra Caverly-Lowery

To my husband Ernest and our son Charles my grateful appreciation for their support and cheerful assistance with this book.

I thank them all for their ceaseless Sacred Acts

Contents

Preface | ix

Chapter 1—**Holy Ground** | 1
Chapter 2—**Can God Come Out To Play?** | 13
Chapter 3—**Artistic Prophecy** | 20
Chapter 4—**What Time Is It?** | 25
Chapter 5—**Planting Seeds of Hope Together** | 33
Chapter 6—**Road Trip** | 40
Chapter 7—**Timeless Stories, Sacred Acts** | 44
Chapter 8—**Meditative Silence** | 51
Chapter 9—**Light and Shadow** | 56
Chapter 10—**Fire and Passion** | 66
Chapter 11—**What's In A Name?** | 72
Chapter 12—**Creative Juices** | 79
After-word | 89

Tips for Making Shadow Screen and Shadow Puppets | 91
Suggested Further Reading: | 99
Music Resources | 100

Preface

THIS IS A BOOK of and about liturgies—in our families, among our friends, at work, worship and play. Sacred ceremonies move us from chaos to cosmos time after time, throughout history and into the present,

Liturgy is a communal response to the sacred. The term liturgy in Greek means "work of the people" or "public service" as it is the participation of the people in the work of God.

From archaic times rituals in liturgies have given form and meaning to our actions. They mark the holiness of the time and space that surrounds us; they provide a celebration of our joys, and a healing balm for our griefs and despairs.

This book presents an historical perspective of ritual and liturgy and each chapter offers descriptions of creative ceremonies ancient and modern. Some of these liturgies are ecumenical services of worship and others are nonreligious spirit - filled events.

Through delving into ancient practices and timeless stories the reader will come to appreciate how the sacred, marked by ritual, has always been a basic reality in life. And s/he will reflect on the need for a numinous yet earthy awareness of today's social and environmental changes.

Can God Come out To Play is a practical resource that explores the value of ritual and ceremony and shares some of the author's liturgical experiences and designs.

This book is aimed at those who are looking for a spiritual approach to today's challenges and are interested in imaginative

PREFACE

forms and methods to guide them. Educators, divinity students, clergy, event facilitators, environmentalists and care workers will appreciate this book as a valuable resource. And all its readers will have one thing in common—a willingness to recognize God as their mysterious, playful companion.

CHAPTER 1

Holy Ground
Location, location, location!

SACRED OR HOLY GROUND has been at the center of our belief systems since archaic times and in those times the world defined reality as that which was sacred. Mercia Eliade, in his seminal book, *The Myth of the Eternal Return*, discusses our earliest concepts of holy ground. He tells us that there is a series of archaic beliefs which refer to the prestige of the center and of the cosmic mountain. He writes,

"The architectonic symbolism of the center may be formulated as follows:

1. The sacred mountain—where heaven and earth meet—is situated at the center of the world.

2. Every temple or palace, and, by extension, every sacred city or royal residence is a sacred mountain, thus becoming a center.

3. Being an axis mundi (world pillar) the sacred city or temple is regarded as the meeting point of heaven, earth, and hell.
    Paradise, where Adam was created from clay, is, of course, situated at the center of the cosmos. Paradise was the

'navel' of the Earth and, according to a Syrian tradition, was established on a mountain higher than all others. And Adam was created at the same spot where the cross of Christ was later to be set up. The same traditions have been preserved by Judaism."

This symbolism has survived in the Western world down to modern times; the idea that the sanctuary symbolically reproduces the Celestial Jerusalem. The symbolisms of the mountain, the Ascension, and the quest for the center are clearly found in novels and other literary works written through the centuries. In fact, in war-torn mountainous regions today, people take refuge on the ancient high ground not just for strategic advantage but for protection by the sacred mountain of their ancestors. One might also say that the continual effort of architects to outdo each other in designing the tallest building in the world is an ongoing quest for the cosmic mountain!

As we travel and take in the remarkable beauty of our Earth, viewed from a mountain, seaside, city, and even from space she continues to represent the sacred and the real. She performs her liturgies quietly in the community of sun, rain and when we are not looking, snow. Insects, birds and those of us who love gardening join this nurturing congregation to produce beauty, shade and the food that sustains us. Earth is teeming with life and it literally holds us up. We evolved from her and we shall return to her.

The Earth and all her living beings, including humans are intrinsically connected, like an arm to a shoulder or a branch to a tree. Most of us are not really aware of how interconnected we are to all life. This lack of awareness can make us indifferent and dispassionate toward the nonhuman life with whom we share the planet. We are now able to see the dire consequences of human societies' self-absorbed worldview. I believe we are desperately in need of a paradigm shift which moves us from feeling that we are on the Earth to knowing we are of the Earth and to regard all life as subject not object. There are those trying to see this wholeness even while, as a species, we are still struggling just to accept one another!

HOLY GROUND

Perhaps a first step for individuals in broadening our horizons to see ourselves as of the Earth and to gain a glimpse of holy ground could be to take a walk! When faced with a problem the expression, "Put on your hat and go for a walk" is well-founded, holistic advice as it involves both the body and an initial commitment. So, breathe deeply and experience the sun the rain the snow or the night sky. Include a sense of the numinous through prayer or sacred awareness. Try walking a two mile round trip, or whatever distance suits your body, and become intimately acquainted with your neighborhood—cats, dogs and their walkers, trees and plants (as they move through their cyclical changes) architecture and the details of the landscape. Allow your mind to wonder and your creative juices to flow as, with senses alert, you breathe and walk. Do this ritually, the same route and at regular intervals—daily, weekly or even monthly. As you gain an at-oneness with the life on your familiar route, you may find, in time, that a problem is solved or a creative idea born and that you, in your retoned body, are walking on holy ground.

Here is a liturgy I originally created for the United Church of Canada. It is a more fully detailed liturgy than others in this book as it includes a children's time, youth event, sermon outline, designated prayers and the description of a new sacrament. This is a slightly rewritten version with basic liturgical directions to make it more accessible to all and to provide a reference for some of the liturgies that follow. It was one of the first Eco-theology liturgies designed for the United Church's liturgical Season of Creation which is celebrated in September. It could easily be adapted to a nonchurch setting. Though intended for a Christian community, I believe that with a few changes in wording any sacred gathering concerned with the future of our Earth could feel at ease with this liturgy.

Creation Centered Liturgy

Opening Prayer

Leader: We gather together, Gracious Provider, in your presence, to celebrate our oneness with the earth and to beg her forgiveness for the injuries we have caused. Help us to hear the voices of our prophets and give us the will and the compassion to respond through you with healing action. Amen

Hymn of Praise—Kelly Walker's, *Hymn To Mother Earth* [see Music Resources at the back of this book]

Exchange of The Peace

Leader: Let us exchange the Peace with one another.
The peace of God be always with you.

Congregation: And also with you.
(Exchange of the Peace—a hug or a handshake with the people around you saying, "Peace be with you.")

Children's Moment—(See Children's Talk under Suggested Directions...)

Readings:

Epistle—1st Timothy 6:6-19 (New Revised Standard Version—NRSV)

Gospel—Luke 16:19-31 NRSV (Done as one person mini-drama. See Suggested Directions...)

Sermon (See Suggested Directions . . .)

(Long Silence—2 minutes—could play *Be Still And Know That I Am God* from the CD *Songs of Presence*.)

Prayers Of The People

Led and composed by a layperson who will incorporate the worship theme while praying for:
The Church
The world
The community
The sick and those in need
Thanksgiving for the lives of those who have died.

End with a two to four line prayer of thanksgiving written or found by the prayer presenter. (If possible this should be led from the nave or the midst of the gathering).

Confession

Leader: Let us confess our human failings to The One on whose grace and mercy we depend saying,

We, like the Rich Man, ignore the cries of the prophets of today. We have not heard them add their voices to Moses and the prophets of old, imploring us to repent and change our self-serving ways. We have shown indifference to the many species disappearing from our midst, the perforation of our fragile atmosphere, the deadly pollution of our waters. We have not cared for the starving, sore covered earth, the Lazarus, at our gates. All-powerful God of the Cosmos, forgive us and inspire in us the imagination to redefine ourselves as creatures of the Earth—soil of your soil. Grant us, Creator God, the wisdom to hear your prophets, to know that all pain is our pain and all joy is our joy as we work to restore your beautiful world. Amen

(Silence)

Kyrie Eleison (sung)
Congregation:
Kyrie eleison
Christe eleison
Kyrie eleison

Assurance of Pardon

Leader: Holiest Hope, we trust in your great love and mercy that though we have practiced greed and shortsighted ambition you will grant us forgiveness of our sins. We feel your presence as you guide us along your holy ground to regain our place as partners with all the earth. And we breathe your love through the love we give and receive from one another. Amen

The Offering: (during which *Soil of God, You and I* #174 in *More Voices* is sung by the congregation).

Leader: (when offering is presented) The gifts of God for the nurture of the Earth.
Congregation: Thanks be to God.

Prayer of Thanksgiving and Supplication

Leader: O Being of Infinite Wonder, we thank you for the beauty and true riches of the Earth. We delight in your image shown in the trees, waters, stars, the song of a bird, a creature's touch, the scent of rain. We are grateful for the ebb and flow of our lives from joy to grief and back to joy again. Like the hairs on our heads our blessings are too numerous for anyone but you to count. Though the Earth is small in your shining Universe and we humans are but stardust in your grand design, we live in the knowledge of your love and protection. Only with your help may we conjure back your glorious vision. Amen

Leader: You are invited to make your way to the table in the center aisle to receive God's blessing through one another with earth and water as a reminder of our oneness with all life.

Community Blessing

(Children rejoin the whole community at this time)

Kum Ba Yah (With new lyrics—see Suggested Directions . . .) (While congregation sings this they will move to the Community Blessing Table in the center aisle—see Suggested Directions . . .)

(Silence after all have received a blessing.)

Hymn of Departure *This Is God's Wondrous World* #296 *Voices United.*

Commissioning for Mission or Dismissal

Leader: Let us go out into the world renewed by the Holy Spirit, and strengthened for action by this community.

Congregation: Thanks be to God or Amen.

Suggested Directions and Information for this Service of Worship.

Set up:

Set a small table (or two if the population is large) in the midst of the community. Place an attractive bowl of earth, a container of water, and a candle (which will be lit at the beginning of the service) on the table. It is important that this table be placed in the midst of the worshiping community to remind us of our connection with the Earth. The elements on this table will also be used during the service.

Youth Involvement:

A weekend or two before this worship service have the community's youth view Al Gore's DVD, *An Inconvenient Truth* with discussion about our human role in the Universe. Borrow a cottage for an overnight youth excursion taking a digital camera and someone who knows the constellations. The youth could learn about and enjoy the sky while taking photos in various directions and at different times through the night. These photos could be developed/printed and enlarged to provide a display in the chancel or around the church on the day of the worship service (or throughout a designated Creation Season). The youth could also draw or find a picture of the globe, reduce it on a photocopier to as small a size as possible and glue copies of this onto the photos of the night sky.

Directions for Mini-Gospel Drama:

(A good resource for basic acting skills which includes memorization, can be found in my book, *We The Storytellers* published by WIPF and Stock in 2013.)

The Gospel storyteller first memorizes the Gospel. The teller, in his/her mind's imagination will place Abraham & Lazarus to one side of him/herself and at a distance. Place the Rich Man to the other side near-by. Visualize these three characters as clearly and in as much detail as possible—their clothing, their postures, their surroundings etc. The more clearly the teller sees these invisible characters the more clearly they will be "seen" by the congregation. Use character voice for the Rich Man and for Abraham and the teller's usual voice for the narrator. If the Rich Man is on the teller's left, he will always look off and to the right when speaking to Abraham. Abraham will always look to the left to speak to the Rich Man. On the narration lines the teller will look straight ahead at the congregation. If no one wishes to take on this bit of drama, the text can be presented as a dramatic reading with the same staging. This Gospel story is the lens through which we look at creation on the day of this worship service.

Directions for Community Blessing and for New Lyrics of *Kum Ba Yah*:

Following the Prayer of Thanksgiving the hymn of faith is introduced. If led by a cantor this is a kind of mantra that people can sing without books or paper. The worship leader or designated person will go to the elements table first and the people can be invited to make their way to the table, row by row such as they might go to a station in a communion service. As the music of *Kum Ba Ya* begins the worship leader puts a pinch of earth into the outstretched hand of the first person saying, "We are the Earth, we are one." Then she/he dips a finger into the water and touches the finger to the person's forehead saying, "We are water, we are one. The receiving person then performs the actions and words to the Worship Leader who then returns to his/her seat. That first receiving person then performs the actions and words again to the next person who then does this for the next and so on until all are blessed each receiving and then blessing another. (This intimacy with earth may offend some adults but getting past this offence is the point!) After people receive and give these elements and blessings they continue down the center aisle and around to their seats singing some or all of the following verses to the tune of *Kum Ba Yah*:

>With your blessing Lord
>We are one
>With your blessing Lord
>We are one

With your blessing Lord
We are one
O Lord we are one

In your rivers Lord . . .
In your orchards Lord . . .
In your mountains Lord . . .
In your oceans Lord . . .
In your cities Lord . . .
In your dreaming Lord . . .
In your mystery Lord . . .
In your cosmos Lord . . .
In your Spirit Lord . . .
And / or any other onenesses you wish

Background For Sermon:

In this service the Gospel is a creation metaphor with Lazarus representing the suffering Earth—the Rich Man as the developed world—Moses and the Prophets as the scientists, ecologists and artists, our prophets of today. These prophets try to warn us of the consequences of our life styles and choices regarding the survival of the Earth. The "fixed chasm" (or hell) of today might be the inherent impossibility of saving the soul of another or of expecting another to gain our salvation for us. Any parent knows the longing to save one's child from stepping into the chasm of making mistakes, bad choices or suffering of any kind. But, we and our children must find our own way, with God's help, to cross the chasm.

This service has been viewed through the lens of the message of this Gospel's call to repent and to take seriously the pain of the Earth community. The goal is to encourage worshipers to see themselves as being of the Earth not on the Earth and to view all life as subject not object.

As a review of the theme I recommend reading any books by the theologian, Thomas Berry and the physicist, Bryan Swimm and for good scientific information the very easy to read small book (also on audio disk), *An Inconvenient Truth* by Al Gore.

Children's Time

Preparation:

Find a large map of the world and glue it to a piece of Bristol board. Draw lines to create a jigsaw puzzle of the map on the back of the Bristol board.

After calling the children to the front, say or paraphrase the following:

The Universe is like a great big jigsaw puzzle of living pieces—sun, moon, stars, planets, water, wind. And our Earth is one small piece of that puzzle. The Earth itself is also a jigsaw puzzle made up of even smaller pieces (show the map—front and back). Can we name some of those pieces? (Animals, people, trees, flowers, insects, birds, fish, rocks, hills—you could burst out with, *The Hills are Alive With the Sound of Music* if you feel inclined)

When all these living pieces of the Earth are in place, together they are one. And each living being is a tiny but vital piece of the whole. What happens when a piece of a jigsaw puzzle is missing? The puzzle is no longer whole. Some pieces from our larger body the Earth are already missing. Can anyone name some? (Dinosaurs, and ice caps melting from global warming and . . .) and some are almost gone (Bald Eagle, and polar bear . . .). Each living being is connected to the whole and is equally important to all and to God.

Let us pray:

Thank you Creator God for our beautiful body the Earth. Teach us to care for our Earth as we wish to be cared for ourselves. Feed us with hope for the future and bring healing to all our living parts. We know that your love and protection are with us always, through Jesus Christ we pray. (Children go to Church School)

In class the jigsaw pieces are cut out and shuffled. Children can draw a living being—animal, person, flower, etc, on the map side of each piece. Then put the puzzle together again on another piece of Bristol board. When the puzzle is assembled apply a spot of glue under each piece and press it into place. Display in public area when finished. Ask the class to come up with a title for this map of the World picture.

Chapter 2

Can God Come Out To Play?
Spirituality is rooted in Earthiness

Contrasts and opposites, the stuff of dramatic art and of story surprise us and give us a new slant on what we thought we knew. The contrasts in a paradox will often help us glimpse truth. A statement like spirituality is rooted in earthiness does not ring true to the Christians who traditionally think of spirituality as otherworldly, beyond the concerns of the body and the activities of daily life.

As a Christian, think for a moment: whom do you consider a really spiritual person? What images come to your mind? A loud spoken man in his undershirt holding a can of beer and telling an off color joke? A woman who sleeps in every Sunday morning, after a hard week's work, instead of going to church? On the surface, probably neither of these examples strikes us as spiritual. But our roots are in Judaism and their spirituality is grounded in the sensual, the earthy, and in humor, laughter and play. Quite simply their spirituality is rooted in God's creation. To quote an early Jew, from the NRSV, Jeremiah (31:12–14):

> "They will come and shout for joy on the heights of Zion,
> They will throng toward the good things of Yahweh; corn

and oil and wine, sheep and oxen; their soul will be like a watered garden, they will sorrow no more.

The virgin will then take pleasure in the dance, young men and old will be happy; I will change their mourning into gladness, comfort them, give them joy after their troubles"

As Matthew Fox reminds us,

"Jewish thinking which is biblical thinking and which was also Jesus' thinking takes it for granted that the sensual is a blessing and that there is no (spiritual) life without it. To recover a sensual spirituality is to recover a biblical one."

I doubt that we Christians would dream of making earthy prayers like this to God.

"If you think you can bring your people back into the fold by making them suffer, then I, Leib, son of Rachel, swear to you that you will not succeed. So why try? Save your children by giving them joy, by delivering them. By doing it that way, you have nothing to lose and everything to gain."

Or this from a victim of Hitler's persecution:

"Lord, four thousand years ago, on the slopes of Mount Sinai, you chose the Jews as a people peculiar unto you, a holy people, a nation of priests, to bear the yoke of your holy Law and to serve as witness to all the world. Lord, I am deeply sensible of the honor, but Lord, enough already! Surely it is time that you chose somebody else."

Or, finally, from another Jewish prayer,

"We shall give you our sins and in return you will grant us your pardon. By the way, you come out ahead. Without our sins, what would you do with your pardon?"

I don't mean to imply that all Christians are deadly serious or that we eliminate humor in our worship and other dealings with God. It's just that we could look for God in less pious places more often and include playmate as one of God's many roles in our lives. We can demystify God without loosing any of God's mystery. In fact, there is an ancient Russian Orthodox tradition of telling jokes all day on the day after Easter, in Church and out. In this tradition they felt they were imitating that cosmic joke that God pulled on Satan in the resurrection. Satan thought he had won and was smug in his victory, smiling to himself, having had the last word, so he thought. Then God raised up Jesus from the dead, and life and salvation became the last words. And the whole world laughed at the devil's discomfort. This attitude passed into the medieval concept of hilaritas, which did not mean mindless giggling; it meant that even at the moment of disaster one may wink because he or she knows there is a God.

When we pause to laugh and enjoy the moment; reflect and appreciate life's ironies even in the midst of despair we feed our creative imaginations. The contrast or paradox of laughter in the midst of pain or injustice can redirect our thoughts and feelings, even if only slightly, onto a more hopeful path.

Here is a story that I think exemplifies this point. It was written by the Rev. Craig Boly. I have told this story at a funeral followed by Kelly Walker's lovely hymn, *Paradise* (See Music Resources). This story serves well as a homily, in the narrative style, and I love its hopeful message and its playful concept.

On Death by Rev. Craig Boly S.J.

Once upon a time, life began for twins in their mother's womb. The spark of life glowed until it caught fire with the formation of their embryonic brains. With their simple brains came feeling, and with feeling a sense of surroundings, of each other, of self.

When they perceived the life of each other, they knew that life was good and they laughed and rejoiced, the one saying,

"Lucky are we to have been conceived, and to have this world." And the other chimed,

"Blessed be the Mother who gave us this life and each other."

Each budded and grew arms and fingers, lean legs and stubby toes. They stretched their lungs, churned and turned in their newfound world. They explored their world, and in it found the life cord which gave them life from the precious Mother's blood. So they said,

"How great is the love of the Mother, that she shared all that she has with us."

And they were pleased and satisfied with their lot.

Weeks passed into months, and with the advent of each new month they noticed a change in each other, and changes in themselves.

"We are changing," said the one. "What can it mean?"

"It means," said the other, "that we are drawing near to birth."

An unsettling chill crept over the two, and they both feared, for they knew that birth meant leaving all their world behind. Said the one,

"Were it up to me, I would live right here forever."

"But mightn't there be a life after birth?" asked the other.

"How can there be life after birth?" cried the first. "Do we not shed our life cord and also the blood tissues? And have you ever talked to one who has been born? Has anyone reentered the womb after birth? No!"

The first of the two fell into despair and in this despair moaned,

"If the purpose of conception and all our growth is that it must be ended in birth, then truly our life is absurd."

Resigned to despair the one stabbed the darkness with unseeing eyes, and clutched the precious life cord saying,

"If all this is so and life is absurd, then there really can be no Mother."

"But there is a Mother." protested the other. "Who else gave us our nourishment and our world?"

"We get our own nourishment and our world has always been here. And if there is a Mother, where is she? Have you ever seen her? Does she ever talk to you? No! We invented the Mother because it satisfied a need in us. It made us feel secure and happy."

Thus while one raved and despaired, the other became resigned to birth, and placed all trust in the hands of the Mother. Hours ached into days and days fell into weeks and it came time. Both knew their birth was at hand, and both feared what they did not know. As the one was the first to be conceived, this one was the first to be born, the other following after.

They cried as they were born into the light. And coughed out fluid and gasped in the dry air. And when they were sure they had been born, they opened their eyes for the first time, and found themselves cradled in the warm love of the Mother. They lay open-mouthed, awe-struck before the one they could only hope to know.

Feast of Fools Liturgy

Here is the outline of a seriously playful liturgy. It is a medieval liturgy called Feast of Fools. It was developed in the late twelfth and early thirteenth centuries as a liturgy for the day of circumcision (January 1). This liturgy or feast served as an alternative to the rowdy secular New Years festivities. The intent of the feast was a thanksgiving for the incarnation of Christ. It prescribed role reversals in which the lower clergy presided over divine office and it recalled Mary's joyous affirmation, in the Magnificate, that God "has put down the mighty from their seat and exalted the humble." The "fools" represented those chosen by God for their lowly status. The feast, never widespread, was largely confined to cathedrals in northern France. In the fifteenth century high-ranking clergy who relied on rumor rather than first hand knowledge heard that this feast was disorderly, sacrilegious and obscene. They attacked and eventually suppressed the feast. Since then this liturgy occasionally returns; I know of instances in Great Briton and I produced it in the 1980s at a large Anglican Church in Toronto Canada. The historian, Max Harris, has made a strong defense for this medieval feast or liturgy in his book, *Sacred Folly-A New History of the Feast of Fools* and Harvey Cox used it as a reflection point in his book, *The Feast of Fools—A Theological Essay on Festivity and Fantasy*.

Liturgy of The Feast of Fools—Toronto Revival

The service of Evening Prayer seemed to begin as usual, by the book. However, the choir was dressed in black robes and medieval style hoods when they processed in. The assistant curate brought up the rear wearing a homemade bishop's mitre. The service continued through the singing of the Magnificate, but when this ended there was a rush of energy in the chancel and a child took over the presider's role. Another child stepped out to direct the choir whose members relaxed into playful activities—a yoyo coming out of a pocket here, a peanut butter sandwich there. Children assumed the roles of acolytes and deacon. The liturgy resumed with all the symbols of the mighty being put down from their seats and the humble exalted.

The children prepared for their roles seriously and performed them admirably. This service was followed by a particularly festive social time with gooey feast and fun for all God's fools.

Scripture reading: John 13

Jesus washes his disciple's feet, or the cleansing of the temple story could be told. This is found in Mark 11:15 or any of the other three canonical Gospels, all of which have this story.

Music:

Open with, *Draw The Circle Wide* from *More Voices*
Close with, *Send in The Clowns* from the theatre production, *A Little Night Music.*

Chapter 3

Artistic Prophecy

I HAVE LONG FELT that artists are some of the prophets in today's society. By that I mean that the artist in all of us has the potential for prophesy. Doing art, any art, requires pursuing a vision and taking risks; it seems to me that the biblical prophets had just the same job description. Jesus' followers are to live a prophetic and itinerant life-style on the margins of society which fits most artists rather well. And our liturgies require art and prophesy to inspire thought, feeling and commitment.

But where there are prophets there must be listeners; these are equal roles. As listeners our responsibility is to trust and respond. In Mark 6:4–6 Mark quotes Jesus as saying,

"Prophets are not without honor, except in their hometown and among their own kin and in their own house. And I could do no deed of power there."

It seems that deeds of power come about when the listeners allow themselves to be inspired by the prophet's words and actions. At least half the onus is on the listener. Often we know people too well or we think we know, too much of their personal stories to be able to receive what the Holy Spirit is communicating through them.

ARTISTIC PROPHECY

There could be a workshop exclusively on the art of being an audience—the importance of response. The lecture, sermon or performance grows and develops as a result of the well placed, out-loud laughter or intent silent listening or even the encouraging facial expression given back by the audience. These are symbols of affirmation of the worth and value of the presentation. There is a sense of sacred presence when everyone in a space is focused, affirming and hopeful together.

I have sometimes felt that presence during a service of Communion when I am offered the bread or the cup from someone I ordinarily have little regard for. But when our eyes meet I feel a warmth and compassion toward him and the world at large. My challenge is to find creative ways to keep that feeling alive beyond the return to my pew! That same liturgical experience of compassion or spiritual awareness can happen anywhere—at a social gathering, a business meeting or when encountering a person living on the streets. If we genuinely see and listen we may find we are in the presence of a prophet.

Often the prophet "can do no deed of power there" because our response to prophesy is fear—fear of discomfort—fear of change—fear of the unknown and we are blocked both as prophets and in our response to prophesy.

In liturgical art or Church sponsored theatre we are frequently asked to edit a play, dance, music or visual piece so as not to offend anyone and in life we often edit what is said to us in order to hear only what we want to hear. I'm guessing many biblical prophets would have loved to speak a watered down version of God's "script," Jonah comes to mind and for that matter, Jesus probably, but in the end they spoke the truth as they believed it to be. So that "even when we were a 'rebellious lot' we, at least, knew that there had been a prophet among us" Ezekiel 2:5.

Prophets of old, trusted that their words came directly from God. In fact, some Rabbis didn't allow persons under 30 to read the beginning or the end of Ezekiel because of the danger of probing too deeply into the mysteries.

Can God Come Out To Play?

If artists are some of today's prophets it is because artists generally trust their intuitions and C.S. Lewis's "that other way of knowing." They face and believe in a mystery beyond their understanding and they feel enough passion for their work to be willing to live on the margins of society. I don't think there is such a thing as Christian art and other art—just art whose artists use a variety of different languages to communicate their source of inspiration. To me being an artist today is to dare to express one's deepest beliefs and questions and to find the tools to help those without voice, from oppressed people to endangered species, to be heard—in short to be a prophet. For me now that would be through writing or teaching but there is the opportunity to be an artist in every field.

Art is a process of creating—saying, "Yes" to life. When the spirit meets the heart, mind and hands that is art. Christ the healer is Christ the artist.

Art by definition has always been a process rather than something geared for results. The product of an art—painting, play, dance, composition—is, for both artist and audience, a reflection point that leads to the next experience of art.

Over the centuries art has moved from being perceived as predominately an object of beauty, glorifying in itself, to being a means of consciousness raising, exposing the evils of the world, to the emerging present direction of a partnership art, promoting social action through public communal participation. For example, those who gather to protest inequalities or to support the oppressed are making an art form out of a caring act that gives hope and purpose to those who experience it. The arts, like religion, cannot exist outside and divorced from society.

In order to turn a caring, compassionate act into an art form or artistic liturgy the act needs to include trust (in ourselves and others), ritual (a repeated act of timing or actions that acknowledge spirit), and these actions need to be in relationship with others, people or environment, not done to them. So here is one simple liturgical way that we, as God's play-mates, could all initiate the kind of artistic liturgy we have been talking about—art that is participatory, hopeful, includes ritual, and cleans up after itself!

Outdoors, Art-Centered Liturgy

First we identify an area in our environment that needs to be restored to health—lakeside, riverside, lot, park, alley, or block. We, as artist(s), could commit to going to that unhealthy space with spade and broom or whatever appropriate tools for a given elapsed time at a specified hour each day or once a week or even once a month. We start with prayer (silently or aloud) offering our work to God. And then we begin to make art inviting those who pass by or show interest to contribute suggestions or to participate. We could create a sculpture or puppets from "garbage," or compose music inspired by the surrounding sounds, or prepare a performance, written or improvised, from overheard and observed words and movement, or simply plant a garden. As we clean and beautify the space we might be surprised at the inspirations we will have. We could compose group poetry, freeform or from one of the ancient styles. We might find materials on the site to weave a tapestry or be moved to create a montage of photographs. We could paint a mural or some simple daisies on the side of a shed or old fence (if permitted), or we could create chalk designs on pavement or parking lot. The artist in all of us can do all of these things. Passers-by could contribute to the work directly or to the evolution of it through their comments and suggestions.

At the very least we will be acting out our artistic vision in that space responding to its needs. We will be attempting to demonstrate the community's care and concern for that small piece of the world. "Whether they listen or refuse to listen, for they are a rebellious lot, they shall at least know that there has been a prophet among them." And we can reflect on the experience and let it lead us on to the next.

Chapter 4

What Time Is It?

Here is a story entitled, Don't Change from Song of the Bird by Anthony deMello

> I was a neurotic for years. I was anxious and depressed and selfish. Everyone kept telling me to change.
>
> I resented them, and I agreed with them, and I wanted to change, but simply couldn't, no matter how hard I tried.
>
> What hurt the most, like the others, my best friend kept insisting that I change. So I felt powerless and trapped.
>
> Then, one day, he said to me, "Don't change. I love you just as you are."
>
> Those words were music to my ears: "Don't change. Don't change. Don't change . . . I love you as you are."
>
> I relaxed. I came alive. And suddenly I changed!
>
> Now I know that I couldn't really change until I found someone who would love me whether I changed or not.
>
> Is this how you love me God?

Perhaps the key characteristic of spiritually growing up is compassion—the willingness and ability to love ourselves and others whether we change or not. This is ultimately the true relational stance of allowing ourselves and the other to rest. Brian Swimme, the noted physicist and theologian, has posed the big question that hangs in the air at this time in the evolving of humankind, "Can human beings become a compassionate species?"

Every age brings change. but in the last half-century we humans, have substantially altered our body the earth. We have poisoned all four of her basic elements in a competitive race to acquire more and more personal gain. Possibly, we are running as fast as we can to hide from the future.

But perhaps this race is, even now, breathlessly approaching a finish line, breaking into yet another change.

What time is it?

The hope is that, as a society, we might pass from an adolescent stage of psychological development (the majority of the culture is in this stage) to an adult stage of maturation. As Elisabet Sahtouris (philosopher-scientist of organisms biology) says in her very helpful book *Gaia: The Human Journey From Chaos to Cosmos*:

> "Like any adolescent who is suddenly aware of having created a very real life crisis, our species faces a choice—the choice between pursuing our dangerous course to disaster or stopping and trying to find mature solutions to our crisis. This choice point is the brink of maturity—the point at which we must decide to continue our suicidal competitive economics and politics, our ravaging of the environment, or to change our worldview, our self-image, our goals, and our behaviour in accord with our new knowledge of living nature in evolution. It is the point at which we can see our own historical evolution and decide whether to continue opposing it with old hostilities or whether to speed its evolution into a mature cooperative body of humanity by conscious choice."

This choice point at the brink of maturity is as relevant individually as it is globally. The choices and eventual changes we make in our daily lives are what matter. They, when multiplied, have the potential to transform the planet. To begin, can we make a concerted effort to love ourselves and others whether we change or not?

What Time Is It?

Through liturgy we can look at this and other urgent questions as liturgy tells our timeless story; its rituals guide the sacred moments of our lives and always have. From the beginning of recorded history we have felt compelled to repeat our mysterious and hopeful stories as these enact the original acts of God or the gods. The only profane activities are those which have no mythical meaning, that is, those that lack exemplary models. Thus from the archaic world to the present we might say that every responsible, repeated activity in pursuit of a definite end is a ritual. These priceless repeated acts enfolded in our life liturgies are as necessary to humans as food, sleep and creative imagination.

To strive for compassion or for any worthwhile goal requires creativity. We all have creative imagination in us but artists tend to model it by making it the focus of their work as well as their play.

Robert Janz, born in Belfast in 1932 is one of Ireland's most celebrated artists. He is a painter, sculptor, performing artist, and print maker. Always on the move through Europe, the United Kingdom, and the United States he creates his art both indoors and outdoors. His works are explorations of and comments on aspects of motion and change—what time is it?

Some of his work, such as his water drawings on rocks, are his way of showing the transience of all life. He has chronicled the life span of flowers, sequentially, through arcs of time and the processes of their budding, blooming and decaying. He says, " . . . the life of a flower is a compact summary of mortality." Robert invites us to look at whole time not just the present time. To him the flower is the voice of the land speaking. Through his art Robert hopes to increase our awareness of the fragile state of our environment and our opportunity for choice. His performances are the actions of creating and recreating his visual art. He draws, erases and redraws; paints and repaints, continually changing the space. His audiences experience the performance of this evolution.

My mind, from time to time, turns to life changes and the probability of outliving my husband, he is much older than I. His death would be the death of the life liturgy that I know and love. However, I take some comfort from the many people who have survived this erasing and somehow slowly adapted to their redrawn lives. I can't avoid the grief that is to come but I can try to develop some tools to deal with it. One of the things that Ernest and I share is humor. We recognize the same ironies and laugh at the same things. I can take this from the liturgy of our life together and build on it through memories and new stories. Ernest prepares for my future by taking opportunities to casually mention his appreciation of me. He knows these generous comments are creating memories for me of our loving relationship. We can't prepare for our own life-to-come as it is beyond our concept but we can do our utmost to make the changes and lost rituals easier for those we love.

Liturgical Event for the theme of time:

It has been said that those who pay no attention to history are destined to repeat their mistakes.

An Anglican Church in Canada, where I was invited to be an educational resource person, was celebrating its historical landmark of 125 years. "Only by North American standards would this brief period of time be considered historical!" I quote my Englishman husband.

A great effort was made to get as many members of the parish as possible to attend this workshop day. The parish had new members as well as oxygenarians who had attended the church all their lives.

The task of the day was to ask themselves, "What time is it in this parish church and in our lives together?"

In addition to worshipping and eating together they devised a process for the morning of mapping time and telling stories. A wide roll of paper was attached to the walls around the large gathering space. The paper was divided, with markers, into 10 decades with lots of space for writing. The people were invited to gather around the decade space that marked their original, individual arrivals at that church. They took time to look around and note the flow of people entering their church over the years.

This was truly an all-age event so careful thought was given to accessibility, appropriate refreshments and a variety of comfortable seating. The decade groups then settled in to reflect together and tell the stories of their arrival decade. Some remembered when women had to cover their heads to enter the sanctuary, some mentioned the lack of iconography, not even a processional cross, "back then" and others spoke of the warm welcome their children were given. Still others, who had only joined this community recently, remarked that their crying baby had been resented. Another told the story of how a pregnant woman who had just arrived from another city chased her down the street after the service saying, somewhat breathlessly, "You've been so thoughtful to us since we arrived. I've been trying to catch you for the past three weeks but you get away before I have a chance. We've decided to have our baby baptized here and make this our church home—will you be Jimmy's Godmother?"

As they storied, they noted on the decade paper the events, impressions and feelings they experienced coming to this parish. After an hour of comfortable storytelling each group shared its history high/low lights with the whole gathering. Then in whole group they began to discuss what time they felt it was in the parish right now. In preparation for this a statistical descriptive list of the parish family was projected on a screen so that they could look at who they were, collectively—number of children, youth, adults, seniors, country/city of origin, new comers, "old" timers. They then listed, on flip chart the programs the parish currently mounted in worship, education, community building and outreach. They considered what effect their facilities and location had on their programs and their community at large. Were there groups or individuals who were intentionally or unintentionally excluded from their programs? In new small groups they were asked to make a list of the parish community's strengths and a list of its weaknesses using words, drawings and short phrases. And finally these small groups were asked to compose a one sentence description of the parish as it is at the moment and to be specific and honest with no excuses and no "motherhood and the flag phrases." All was recorded. The small group discussions with lists and the parish descriptions were viewed with questions and answers in the whole group and the process flowed into lunch.

In the afternoon everyone looked at the morning's material, particularly the lists of strengths and weaknesses. In small groups they applied themselves to designing a list of goals for the parish attaching a reasonable time line where possible. A date was set for another gathering / meeting approximately two weeks hence, to take advantage of the momentum, to discuss the how and when these goals might be accomplished. All were strongly urged to attend the next meeting where the precious decade paper and flip chart papers would be put up again and briefly reviewed. Any research deemed necessary at this meeting would be reported on at the next.

The day was punctuated with energy snacks and the opportunity for five-minute stretch exercises. It began with a 20 minute commitment worship service when the scripture, "To everything there is a season" Ecclesiastes 3:1–8 was read and reflected upon by the leader with contributions from the group. They ended the opening service with the song, *Day By Day* from the theatre production, *Godspell*.

There was a 20-minute closing service of thanksgiving for the work of the day and its continuing commitment. A prayer encompassing the specific work of the day and the goals for the future was composed by everyone present as an interactive prayer: A table, piled high with large (3–4 inch) Lego blocks, a stack of postit notes and a box of felt pens, was set up in the room where it would not have to be moved for the foreseeable future. As people assembled for the closing service each participant picked up one Lego block, a pen and a Postit Note pack. A medley of "time" songs was played, which included Day By Day and Four Seasons (see Music Resources) as everyone assembled. The designated leader then called for brief, positive reflections of the day from everyone—"I loved that Mary was able to stay all day" "The stories this morning reawakened the enthusiasm I had for this community 40 years ago." When all who wished to had spoken the leader began the prayer with:

"Gracious God we thank you for this time together, this time that is now. Sustain and strengthen us as we look outside ourselves to see those in need. Help us to feel the compassion for others and for creation that you feel for us and to put those feelings into actions.

Through Christ our Lord, Amen "

Leader: "As a symbol of our intention to mark this time as a season of love, peace and growth we create this sculpture together. Your guidance and care, God of all creation, will sustain us as we strive for our hopes and goals."

Can God Come Out To Play?

The leader invited each worshiper to print a hope or goal on a postit, press it to their Lego block and bring it to the table. Each person connected her block to another allowing the sculpture to form under no one's individual design but in its own mysterious way. During this process they sang (with a cantor, the chorus of Kelly Walker's, *Four Seasons*) The service ended with the exchange of the Peace and this dismissal,

Leader:
"Go in peace to think, pray and act out our intentions of today until, God willing, we return on (date in 2 weeks).
People: Thanks be to God."

Chapter 5

Planting Seeds of Hope Together

According to Iroquois legend, corn, beans and squash are three inseparable sisters who only grow and thrive together.

It seems to me that the seeds of hope, love, and personal growth can also only develop through community. Alone time is essential for meditation, personal reflection and daydreaming, but working, playing and creating in community provides a mirror for our souls.

Plants and creatures, including humans, are created as parts of a whole and without moving in and out of communal interaction we can easily slip into self obsession and despair—literally fall apart.

We all see the perfection of Earth's design, not static but constantly recreating to meet her needs through evolution. Perhaps our true role in life is to use our minds and actions to be God's co-creators. This requires the acceptance of ideas that are new to us and sometimes even the promotion of revolution.

I think of the Occupy Movement which has swept a good part of the world in recent years. This movement is the international branch of the Occupy Wall Street movement that protests against social and economic inequality around the globe. The Occupy Movement is driven by individuals coming together to create change from the so-called "bottom" up. Various faith groups have become involved in this movement in the last few years and, of course, there will always be groups and individuals who will object to this world-wide "Feast of Fools" and what it stands for. To me it is a creative and courageous life liturgy that gives voice to the disempowered.

The publication, Yes! Magazine seems to be the best source of ongoing information on this movement.

The Occupy Movement invites radical change. Often we feel that suggested resolutions to enormous problems are too big to contemplate and nothing short of a miracle will make them work. But perhaps the real miracle is that, though we are some times discouraged, we do continue to strive for something close to our full potential.

Here's a story that Christians will recognize; it is told, with variations, in all four Gospels. I tell it here from memory but with some embellishment. I think of it as a story of generosity and sharing that led to transformation.

The Feeding of the Five Thousand

> The rumor spread quickly that the wise preacher they had all heard about would be in the vicinity the very next day. Everyone fervently hoped this was true—some from need, some from curiosity, some from life-long dreams. So as the sun rose on that morning, people from all round the countryside packed a few provisions and gathered children, dogs, blankets, the items they might need for the day and could carry on the journey to the hopeful hillside. They arrived from numerous directions, thousands of them, many tired from walking a long distance. But there he was with a couple of friends and the people settled on the wide expanse of soft grass ready and willing to take in his every word. He spoke and they listened with rapt attention for hours. The sun traveled up and over their heads then slowly slid down to the horizon announcing a blazing reminder of their need for food and refreshment. There were no markets or shops near by from which to buy food but one little boy had dutifully

bought loaves and fishes for his mother along the way. He took them to the preacher, who received this offering and looked up to heaven and blessed it. The boy gave the loaves and fishes to be shared as far as they would go.

Those on the hillside grumbled with hunger, some hoarding and hiding their meager provisions. But as the preacher and his friends distributed the small offering of loaves and fishes the others began, gradually, to share their own bits of bread, dried fruit and water with those around them. As generosity took hold the hillside became a temporary village in itself. Strangers comforted crying children, assisted the elderly and shared what they had. Eventually, all had had enough morsels to sustain them. In fact, there was food left over and gathered for another day.

A Living Liturgy

Here is a description of an ongoing life liturgy that reflects the biblical story above.

I am on the board of directors of the Anglican Foundation of Canada, a fine and generous organization that functions like a caring community. A while ago an intriguing project proposal came our way for support. It was from the Anglican parish of All Saint's Memorial Church, Entry Island. This is a remote island within the Magdalene Islands, reachable only by a ferry from Cap-Aux-Meules, Quebec. This hardy community of 62 people is mostly made up of descendants of shipwreck survivors.

Entry Island's ambitious project, All Saint's Gardens, is an ecclesiastically based community farm where the people are attempting to re-establish their food sovereignty and develop a local, sustainable food system.

For the past few decades lobster fishing has employed 90% of the inhabitants for a few months of the year with unemployment insurance providing the rest of their income.

Historically, the community was self-sufficient socially and in food and other necessities. This ceased only a few decades ago when high lobster prices, in combination with unemployment insurance being extended to seasonal workers, created a surplus wealth. Instead of continuing to produce their own food, community members began to buy it from the other islands that were supplied by the industrial agricultural complex. As the island entered a consumer economy, its local economy and social networks were devastated. Community members no longer spent significant time helping each other to produce life's necessities. Households became increasingly privatized and individualized, leading to a massive disintegration of community life. Then came a faltering global economy where lobster prices fell and the federal government cut back unemployment insurance.

The community, not having produced their own food for decades, no longer felt they had the necessary local resources to adapt to the changing social and economic situation. Youth, who had known nothing outside consumer culture, were unable to find meaningful lives within the community and left without plans to return.

This sad story is not unique but wait, it gets worse.

The rising temperature of climate change has prevented the ice shelf from forming around the Island, which would protect it from erosion during the worst winter storms. And oil exploration has been proposed off shore, which threatens the remaining fish and shellfish stocks.

All these factors, combined, have created a sense of fear in the Entry Island population which has deepened community conflict, as families fight over increasingly scarce resources. One might say, Entry Island is a microcosm of our evolving global situation in the North Atlantic nations.

However . . . while the future of Entry Island looks grim, it is not without hope. Food sovereignty has existed in living memory. To quote Jeffrey Metcalfe, recent Rector of All Saints Memorial Church and spearhead of the All Saints Gardens project,

> "Many of the skills, tools, and talents of only a few decades ago still exist and just need to be reutilized. The same is true for the local social safety nets that were strongly in place before federal and provincial government programs. In other words, going back to some of the old traditions remains a distinct and perhaps unique possibility for the islanders, and one we believe will breath new life into the community. Moreover, the church is one of the last "common spaces" within the community that has stayed neutral in the local "clan wars" over scarce resources, and so, it may be the only site where a truly inclusive community development plan can be accomplished."

The Islanders will create common spaces and outdoor work projects to recultivate community. And they will explore ways to develop related businesses. For instance, although, as one of the Magdalene Islands, they receive thousands of visitors in the summer, they have no tourist industry.

Obviously, there have already been many, many community meetings and much research to develop the plans for All Saint's Gardens. They have agreed that pesticides will not be used and that where possible only local, rare, endangered seeds/breeds will be grown. Everyone in the Garden shares in the work as far as s/he is able and in the harvest. Anyone can join at any time and share equally in the harvest. Matthew 20: 1–16

This project will take a while to establish and so will be done in phases. But ultimately, they will grow vegetables, including, Gaspe flint corn, an extremely rare, early maturing corn, once grown by the Micmacs. Jacques Cartier observed fields of it in 1534.

The Islanders will breed heritage sheep, and Chanticleer chickens, developed originally by Quebec monks, and large, black Tamworth pigs. They have already established a honeybee sanctuary that will be maintained through low intervention methods, and without chemicals in the hope of breeding resilience back into the endangered bees. I have tasted a sample of the honey and they are definitely doing something right!

They will also build moveable interpretation panels, which explain the animal/plant that is being nurtured and how All Saints' Gardens' methods are different from the industrial agricultural ones. These panels will show how the wisdom from the traditions of Christianity and the indigenous peoples might apply to the nurture of each animal or plant.

Visitors to the island will be provided with a map, (available also on line) that includes all the different fields and displays to which they can hike, creating a self-guided tour, and any money the visitors spend will thus remain on the island. Effectively, this would turn the entire island into a Living Museum, rooted in faith.

I believe these 62 people are planting the seeds, literally, of good food, education, and recovery of community. They are an ecological and life affirming model for us all. All Saint's Gardens on Entry Island is to me the very definition of a life liturgy and a work of the people in progress. I intend to follow this unfolding story of reconciliation between living beings and the land.

I look forward, one day soon, to visiting this island and tasting her three inseparable sisters et al.

Chapter 6

Road Trip

LIFE IS ABOUT JOURNEYS from the birth canal to the cemetery plot and who knows what beyond. Our repeated gestures and ceremonies such as marriage, agricultural practices, registering to vote, all our coming of age moments are the rituals that make our journey real. These are not the hallmarks of our journey they are the journey itself. They are what constitute our reality and are, therefore, holy.

For the archaic mentality, reality manifested itself as force, effectiveness and duration. Therefore, the outstanding reality was, and I would say still is, the sacred as it acts effectively, creates things, and makes them endure.

And underlying all our journeys is the quest for home. With our six senses we seek out those elements of our younger years that remind us of and bring us home. Apparently, even if our sense memories are unpleasant to the point of abusive a part of us longs to return to what is home, unearthing those moments of love and belonging. Perhaps the significance of home and our quest for it is what keeps a faith in eternal life alive.

We continue to repeat the archaic rituals in the twenty-first-century adding more, of course, through technology and other innovations. On average we live longer lives but at a much more rapid pace than our ancestors did, often taking for granted that the tools we use might be obsolete in six months.

However, much of today's technology is patterned on the design of human functioning. We have an amazing variety of "software" in our own bodies and minds. Like our metal-plastic imitators our bodies require ongoing care and redesign to meet changing needs. I believe, as a society, we have reached a point where we must slow down simply to take care of our selves and to remember to care for each other. In fact, as our individual journeys progress into middle and elder years we have the opportunity to model a slower, healthier, more balanced way of life to those of any age.

One extreme way that exemplifies a less hectic journey is the pilgrimage. For many going on a pilgrimage is a way of meditating or thinking through a next step in life. My son has walked the pilgrimage to Santiago de Compestella twice using two different routes through France and Spain. He loves walking and has a great interest in the medieval period. There's nothing like walking nine hundred miles in three months to get in touch with a slice of the ancient rolling countryside.

There is an impressive, celebratory liturgy at the Cathedral of St. James in Compestella for those who complete the journey. But, apparently, the real liturgies often happen at the evening meals in the *refugios* with the companions met along the way (companion means one who breaks bread with another). The shared experience and the opportunity to reflect on it with others can be the word, sacrament and exchange of the peace all rolled into one. And as the pilgrims dismiss from one another to set out again in the morning they are that little bit changed and their journeys are enriched.

An Old Tale

> There were 2 brothers who decided to leave home and journey to another land. In those days before going on a journey you performed a ceremony of cleaning your self thoroughly by washing every part of your body and your heart. Therefore, on the day of the journey, the brothers

went to the river and began washing themselves. They took out their hearts, cleaned them, and laid them on a rock to dry a bit as they scrubbed the rest of their bodies. It was believed that by washing one's heart, particularly before a journey, you allowed yourself to experience that journey purely.

The brothers were playful and always joked around with each other so they started playing diving games. Laughter took hold of them and when they had finished washing they left, forgetting their hearts by the river. They realized this only after they arrived at the new land and couldn't find pleasure, understanding or feeling in the new things that their eyes saw. The older brother touched his chest and recognized that his heart wasn't there. His little brother did the same. They picked up their sacks and started walking back home as fast as they could. When they reached the river, days later, their hearts were still there but the arrival of night and day had altered them and ants had eaten certain parts. The brothers washed their hearts and put them back in their places but they could no longer experience things the way they had.

So they must find a way to repair their broken hearts by relighting the fire that is dull within them. They should live for that.

That is what happens when old wisdom and new wisdom merge and find room in the young.

And here follows another ancient journey:

The Liturgy of the Labyrinth

The labyrinth is a walking meditation and a path of prayer. Labyrinths are nondenominational and open to all people. The labyrinth has only one path that leads from the outer edge in a circuitous way to the center. There are no tricks to it and no dead ends. Unlike a maze where you lose your way, the labyrinth is a spiritual tool that can help you find your way.

Walking the labyrinth can reduce stress, quiet the mind, ground the body, and open the heart.

Labyrinth designs were found on pottery, tablets, and tiles that date as far back as five thousand years. Many patterns are based on spirals and circles mirrored in nature. In Native American tradition, the labyrinth is identical to the Medicine Wheel and Man in the Maze. The Celts described the labyrinth as the Never Ending Circle and it is also known as the Kabala in mystical Judaism.

Labyrinths can be found in medical centers, parks, churches, schools, prisons, memorial gardens, spas, cathedrals, and retreat centers as well as in people's backyards. Most are constructed out of doors but there are also Labyrinths painted on canvas for use indoors.

You might repeat the following mantra, or another prayer of your choosing, or you might simply allow your body to lead you and your mind to travel where it will.

Mantra:

Be still and know my journey flows
Be still and know my journey heals
Be still and know my journey lives
Be still and know my journey
Be still and know
Be still

And if you prefer music on your labyrinth walk I suggest the CD *All My Life* by Kelly Walker especially the song, *Going Home* (see Music Resources) and / or the Taize CD entitled, *Songs of Taize*, and / or *By My Side* from the theatre production *Godspell*.

CHAPTER 7

Timeless Stories, Sacred Acts

WE ARE OUR STORIES (not a series of numbers, as we might sometimes think). We live our stories and when we die our personal tales are left behind as our legacy. When we talk about ourselves and others it is through stories. At ceremonial occasions like weddings, funerals and other beginnings and endings these parables come to life. We narrate our day or our week when we gather with friends or family. We are a species of language makers who need words to order our thoughts. These words, as they become stories, develop into rituals that give our lives form and draw us repeatedly out of chaos into cosmos. Stories satisfy the thirst in us for being. And if the word is lacking it still exists through symbol and myth.

Language is so much more than words. I think of the languages of artists—dancers, musicians, those who work with clay, paint or wood. And don't all species have language? Surely the birds with their complex and varied "songs" are storying away to each other and the world at large every morning and evening.

I often quote William Bausch, writer and Roman Catholic theologian, "All stories are sacred as long as they contain an element of mystery and end in hope"

Our stories are bigger than we are as individuals; they are communal. Our biggest stories are about relationships with others and nature and most importantly our relationship with God. Those of us who are Christian join others bringing our story-selves to the altar attempting to become one with God through Christ's story and Christ's symbolic body and blood.

Through our stories we can make a difference in the world—a positive or a negative one depending on the amount of truth and compassion our stories (and therefore we) contain.

Here is an epic story written by Joseph J. Juknialis entitled *Bread That Remembers*. It is another way of looking at ourselves as story.

Bread That Remembers

[Simple "stage" directions are included in brackets for the dramatization of this story]

> A long time ago people had not yet forgotten that bread always remembers what is spoken in its presence. Then everyone knew that if goodness was spoken among those gathered around the bread then those who ate that bread would be blessed; and if it was selfish and evil that was spoken why then those who ate the bread would be cursed with cold hearts and hardened spirits.
>
> There were in those days two brothers. Many thought them to be twins for they looked so much alike not only in appearance but in what they did and how they treated others. However, though they were born in the same year, they were not twins, for the older had been born in January and the younger in December of that very same calendar. Their mother had died in giving birth to the younger, and so the two brothers had been raised by their kind and loving father—each reflecting his goodness and gentleness. Perhaps that is why they were thought to be twins by the many who knew them.
>
> One day in early spring, after they had grown to young manhood, yet before either of them had married and left home, their father grew seriously ill. Before the

seeds of that season had sprouted with life the father died, leaving his sons, then, to depend upon their own goodness.

Together the two brothers came before the judge of that land so that the father's will might be unsealed in order that each might receive what the father had promised. The reading of the will revealed equal portions of life for each of the sons. Because the father had loved them both, without favoritism of any sort, each of the sons received half of the farm on which he had been raised.

At this, the elder son grew angry and resentful. He had deserved the greater share, he insisted, for he was the older of the two; and with that he turned away from the judge and from his brother and left them both alone in that chamber of justice.

When the older brother arrived home he sat in anger at the very table where he and his brother together with their father had shared meals and love and life. There at that table, he allowed his anger to unravel more and more. Shattering the gentle stillness which had long been a family member, he spewed curses and hatred at the embarrassed and lonely silence. Suddenly he stood, pounded the table with yet more violence, and left. In all of his anger what the elder brother had never noticed was the bread on the table.

Shortly thereafter the younger brother came home. Having found the elder brother gone, he sat and waited amid the stained silence. When the elder brother never returned the younger brother ate his evening meal alone in the torn darkness of that night.

There he ate the bread which had heard the elder's anger, the bread that remembered. That night the heart of the younger brother grew cold and hardened, scarred with the same selfishness and hatred which lived within the elder.

The next day's morning sun was the sole source of light in the brothers' home. The older brother did return but without the gentleness and love which once were his. So also did the younger brother live without his father's gifts, twinned again, though now in hatred as once they had been in goodness and peace.

During those weeks of summer, the entire countryside came to recognize the change which had come about between the two brothers. Their hearts quietly wept in sadness over that tragic occurrence.

Somewhere in the middle of that summer the wise one of the village invited the inhabitants of the surrounding countryside to a common meeting. On a warm summer evening all but the two brothers came to the village square in the center of the town. Men and women gathered, children came along, strangers were welcomed.

There on the table in the center of their gathering, was placed a single loaf of bread. When it seemed that all had arrived, the one who was wise came before them [Wise Woman enters] and explained why she had called them together.

"If it is true that the bread always remembers, then perhaps we can bring blessings of gentleness and love once again."

She then invited all those who had come, to tell stories of the goodness which once lived in the hearts of both the elder and the younger brother, and to tell those stories in the presence of the bread—the bread that always remembers.
One by one, then, they came forward and stood before the bread and before their neighbours, there to tell their own story of how they had been blessed with life by the two brothers.

*Many stories were told that night all in the presence of the bread. [*This is the cue for the first reader if you are using audience participation]

(Replace the following brackeded text with the lines you have given the participants):

["There were stories of how the two had once taken in a stranger who was sick and lost, and other stories of the time a neighbor had broken a leg at the beginning of the planting season and how the brothers worked nights by moonlight to plant his fields after they had planted their own in order that the neighbor might have crops to harvest come autumn.

Others told stories of how the brothers had shared half of their own harvest with a neighbor when his barn burned and, with the barn, all of that season's labors as well."]

All evening long villagers and country folk stood in front of everyone and, in the presence of that lone loaf of bread, and told stories of the gentleness and goodness which once had made a home among the brothers. When the last story had been told, well past the time when many of the children had fallen asleep in the arms of their parents, all those who had gathered made their way to their homes and to the healing sleep which awaited them.

After all had left, the wise one who had gathered them all stood alone at the table with the bread. There in the summer silence of that night she picked up the loaf of bread, placed it in a sack, and began her journey to the home of the two brothers.

[Wise Woman takes the bread to the altar and places it there.]

She arrived just before the sun, when the nighttime had not yet begun to shed her skin of darkness. Her deed was simple and quickly done—to leave the bag which held the bread at the door and depart.

[Wise Woman returns to her pew.]

As she made her way home amid the early showers of morning sun, she realized she was not tired though she had not slept the entire night. Instead she felt within herself a rising hope of life, fed by the faint possibility that perhaps the two brothers, when they found the bread, might just offer each other that bread and with it all of the goodness and gentleness and love it remembered.

Liturgy with Narrative Homily

I have used the above story as the homily in a Eucharist. So, as a church liturgy, I suggest your usual communion service which could include the prayers, lections, and hymns below.

Place a handsome, homemade loaf of bread on the elements table in the center aisle before the service begins. And write, on slips of paper, individual comments, in first person tense, that begin, "I remember when the brothers . . ." and give one each to a few people in the congregation as they arrive. Choose those with strong voices and ask them to say their line at the appropriate time in the story. Give the first person a cue from the story and the others will follow that person.

Before the Sunday ask an individual storyteller to tell this story as the sermon. Arrange to have an older women in the community enact the Wise Woman when the Wise Woman enters the story and ask her to speak the indicated line. Toward the end of the story she will put the bread in a cloth sack and place it on the altar as directed in the text of the story (" . . . to leave the bag which held the bread at the door and depart").

I suggest the Gospel, Luke 24: 13–35

You may want to use the following as an opening prayer:

"We gather on this day, God of infinite wonder, to strive for goodness through hope and sing praises for your love.
Guide our tongues as we join our stories with Yours.
Keep us from unjust anger
And help us to forgive and be forgiven.
Bless the stories we hear, the stories we tell, and the stories we are.
Through Christ, our everlasting story.
Amen

Music:

Can God Come Out To Play?

You may wish to open with *Gather Us In* # 7 from the United Church's *More Voices* and end with *Deep In Our Hearts* #154 from *More Voices*. As a communion hymn I suggest, *Eat This Bread*, from the *Taize Community, Psalter Hymnal* (Gray) #312

Chapter 8

Meditative Silence

When we dare to be still and listen we can be drawn into the realm of the unknown.

A number of years ago my husband, Ernest, discovered he had a malignant kidney and so it had to be removed. On the day of his operation I was alone in his hospital room from early morning, when he was wheeled out for surgery, until evening when he was returned. I wasn't a patient so I wasn't disturbed by the hospital staff. Out of fear, concern, and love for Ernest, I, quite naturally, concentrated on him completely. I was, unintentionally, meditating. I closed my eyes and entered an intensified waiting time. Eventually, I became aware of total blackness without the little spots and lines of residual light one normally sees with eyes closed. Gradually, the closed-eye landscape of a dark tweed melted into a soft, rich black velvet. I don't know how long this process took—perhaps an hour and a half or two. And then, out of the blackness, a face swam into view. It was not a face I recognized. There was cloth around the head so no hair was visible but the face itself with all its features was clear. Later in the afternoon, as soon as the operation was over, the surgeon came to Ernest's hospital room where he was told I was waiting. He was still in his surgical cap and gown. He said,

"The operation went very well and I was able to examine Ernest closely and found no sign of any other cancer."

I had never met or seen the surgeon, but the face in my meditation was his. My immediate thought was that the clear, clean blackness was the lack of disease his face saw when examining Ernest.

Often I think, in times of anxiety, if we were to focus totally on the situation at hand we could know the outcome. Sometimes we don't attempt that degree of concentration because we are too afraid of what we might learn and sometimes it is because we think we don't know how, but simply trying may be the first step.

In theatre there is a small group or two-person process that we could all use to increase our ability to intensify our attention and perhaps maximize the power of our prayers. It is a problem solving process that can strengthen our adeptness at hearing the voice or seeing the picture that normally lies outside our conscious mind. This process is also used in Neural Linguistic Programming (NLP).

It requires two people. One person is the director, the other the walker.

The walker thinks of a problem—a real problem that he or she has not been able to solve. This is an internal process for the walker; at no time is she/he required to describe or even name this problem out loud. The problem could be a dysfunctional relationship with a co-worker, family member or friend, it could be a daunting or fearful task that looms—a public speaking commitment, a test or evaluation or it could be an awkward or sensitive situation—the need to tell a friend bad news, the need for standing up for one's beliefs when it might not be popular.

Having thought of a problem, the walker mentally puts the problem in a setting and imagines it fully, placing the people involved in a specific and detailed space carrying out a relevant activity.

The walker then places this imaginary scene in an actual spot in the room where this process is being done. The walker moves as far away from the imaginary scene as the room will allow to begin the process.

The director then asks the walker to focus as fully as possible on the imaginary scene and problem, not breaking concentration on it while following the director's verbal instructions.

The director will instruct the walker to walk from the starting point to the imaginary scene and back again repeatedly for about five minutes. All the while the director will call out specific prompts, to alter the walker's posture, gait, or facial expression. These instructions could be lift or lower head, swing arms or hold them to your side, smile or frown, stoop or stand very straight, long strides or short strides or skip etc., etc.

After approximately five minutes allow time for reflection. Was the walker able to maintain focus and concentration? Did s/he gain any insights into the problem situation? For this process to work it is never necessary to disclose the nature or details of the problem. This process can, of course, also be done in pairs in a group where everyone takes a turn at being both walker and director.

While in the UK doing a three-month research project on religious/spiritual drama, I spent some weeks with the Society of Friends (Quakers). For those of you unfamiliar with the origins of this society, I quote Peter Ackroyd from his book, *Rebellion* where he is discussing the times in the 1650s.

> "The Quakers believed that no visible church was necessary and that divine revelation was permitted to every human being . . . . they called each other "saints" or "friends of the truth" but, because of their tremblings and quiverings in worship, they became popularly known as Quakers."

I was for those weeks a resource person to the Friends, floundering in a foreign land attempting to help them produce a full-length original musical. There was a cast of two dozen 14 to 22 year olds augmented by half a dozen theatre specialist leaders. The production was for their annual meeting in Stirling, Scotland where Quakers from all over the UK came together that summer staying in the university accommodation and using the university theatre.

The young adults and their leaders worked every day from 9:00 am until 10:00 pm only breaking for meals. As an Anglican I felt compelled to ask them, "When do we stop for a drink?" They didn't. But for half an hour at the beginning and at the end of each day we all gathered for their silent, waiting worship. I found their liturgies and their dedication to observing them inspiring. The amount of work involved in mounting a two and a half hour original musical—creating or procuring costumes, building sets and props, setting lights and, of course, rehearsals was all consuming, but the worship must go on! In fact one morning the university had failed to unlock the theatre for us which was situated in an enclosed mall with banks, cafes, and shops surrounding it. We always began our day with worship at 9:00! So . . . the cast rounded up chairs from the cafes and placed them in a circle in the public concourse. The candle was lit and the day began as usual!

A Liturgy of Silence

This is how "my Friends" carried out their liturgy:

Everyone pulled chairs into a circle with a lit candle, for focus, on a small table in the center. The Spirit moved someone to take the hand of the person on either side of her and the hand-holding continued around the circle until everyone was connected which was the signal to begin. Occasionally, music was set up to play during the worship but usually it was silent until the Spirit moved some to speak. When approximately half an hour had elapsed, someone would take the initiative to squeeze the hand on either side of him—the squeeze traveled around the circle signifying the end of the worship with the last person saying, "Thank you, Friends."

This was done seven days a week, first thing in the morning, and last thing at night. I found that when I gave myself up to the process and focused my mind it could be quite powerful spiritually and refreshing physically. I resolved, at the very least, to include meaningful silence after scripture, homily/story, or significant music or dance in any liturgies I planned when I returned to Canada. This means a minimum of two, preferably three minutes of silence which for most of us seems a long time. Up to one minute of silence the congregation thinks something has gone wrong! So it is only during the second minute that people begin to relax and surrender to the waiting, worshipful silence.

As mentioned, an alternative to absolute silence in this meditative style of worship can include music.

Some suggestions are:

Abide With Me on Kelly Walker's CD *All My Life* also found in the Anglican hymnal, *Common Praise* #24 or The Taize CD, *Music of Unity and Peace*.

Chapter 9

Light and Shadow

THERE IS A HINDU legend that says,

> "There was a time when all humankind were gods. But they abused that divinity. And so Brahma, god of creation, concluded that people had lost their right to divinity and decided to take it away from them. Wanting to hide it somewhere that humans could not find it, he called a council of all the gods to advise him. Some suggested that they bury the divinity deep in the earth, others advised him to sink it to the bottom of the oceans, still others would have him put it on top of the highest mountain. But Brahma said, humankind is ingenious and would dig down far into the earth, troll the deepest oceans, and climb every mountain in an effort to find it again. The gods were on the point of giving up when Brahma said, I know where we will hide humankind's divinity. We will hide it inside him. He will search the whole world but never look inside and find what is already within."

We each have a shadow side; a side we would rather not show to others but that they invariably see. For a full description of our shadow side read *Everyman*, the morality plays where our seven deadly sins are brought to life!

LIGHT AND SHADOW

Our shadow sides cause us to wear a mask and these masks support the denial of our faults. Our masks can also hinder us in discovering our divinity within—knowing that God is both beyond our reach and deep inside us.

We can develop our unhealthy habits into unwanted rituals as we hide from our faults, refusing to face our weaknesses. We are all prey to our shadow sides and sometimes they are most active hidden away in our minds where we ritually rehearse our negative and angry thoughts. Self-acceptance and forgiveness is necessary before we can discard our masks and shed our unwanted shadows.

This is, of course, an ongoing process as we are all works in progress / imperfect beings. So perhaps there is a balance between confidently facing ourselves and vulnerably hiding. I believe it is necessary to allow the shadows to envelop us in order to walk through them into the light. For Christians Easter is not possible without Good Friday. As we hear in Leonard Cohen's song, *Anthem*,

> "Ring the bells that still can ring
> Forget your perfect offering
> There is a crack in everything
> That's how the light gets in"

Our shadow side is not evil; it is simply a neglected part of us. It could be likened to a film negative (remember those?)—the black and white image that is unfinished and lacks the color and nuance of the developed film. Our undeveloped self is the basis of a story that we can grow into. These black and white negatives occur over and over in our lives and when we allow them to develop into positives they emerge from the shadows as our incarnations.

We change and develop because we are creatures of imagination and that is a magnificent human trait. But imagination alone can take us in many directions including down into despair. However, if we move our imaginations into positive action—create, make, engender, originate or produce—we will be exercising our God given responsibilities to keep this beautiful world going. Therefore, creative imagination is our salvation. In fact, I think creative imagination is the Holy Spirit speaking to us. It has been said, "Where there is creativity there is no despair." Creative imagination can develop our good ideas and intentions and move them out of mere shadows into action.

One form of action appears as inaction—a fallow/Sabbath/pregnant time that can connect us to the unknown—to a power within whom we dwell. By definition fallow time is a time of reflection, of letting go of control, and shortsighted goals. It is a time when we can receive wisdom, healing and guidance from the Holy Spirit through our own creative imaginations.

Fallow time is a vigorous, fertile, and ultimately high-yielding downtime. It is home to creative imagination.

As persons and as a society we have all but dispensed with fallow time in our lives in favor of our masks of super activity. Which of us does not feel at least a little insulted at being thought to have free time? Who do we know who does not take pride in their too numerous to count daily or weekly tasks and responsibilities?

"How are you?"

"Tired. I've been so busy this month I've hardly seen my family. And friends? What friends?"

"Haven't you been on holiday?"

"Well yes, but work goes on you know. Mind you I really did try not to pull out my smart phone more than three times a day."

When we learn to value, design, and incorporate fallow time into ourselves, it becomes an integral part of us and contributes a ritual rhythm and an energy to our lives. We are able to shed many of our addictive patterns, that shadow side of us, that feeds our identities in unhealthy ways.

What follows is a creative liturgy that is actually a theatre production. It is a story of the incarnation. This version moves us from literal shadows (shadow puppets) into the word made flesh.

For those who wish to try a shadow puppet staging of the play, I have included a section with some directions for building a shadow screen and creating shadow puppets. I have also suggested print and electronic resources. However, I recommend that you involve a local puppeteer to provide a workshop on constructing and operating shadow puppets. The essence of all puppetry is movement and if actual puppeteers are involved there could be more moving parts in these puppets than is indicated here. There are puppetry organizations scattered all over North America and beyond.

Liturgy—Evening Performance

The Shepherds (A Christmas Story)

The script is adapted from the original medieval play with modern text by the Rev. Eugene Kellenbenz O.S.B.

I have staged this play with shadow puppets and added a final scene with live actors that brings the Christmas story into today.

Some of you may want to read the section of this book entitled, Tips for Making Shadow Screen and Shadow Puppets, now, before reading the play to be better able to visualize it.

Puppet Characters/Items:

(In order of appearance)

(Several characters are combined into one puppet for easier manipulation)

- Groundscape—A solid, slightly rolling groundscape, a few inches high. It is attached to both sides of the frame and runs across the width of the bottom of the screen and remains there throughout the play. It is the ground on which the puppets move or sit.
- Stained Glass Window—Nearly covers screen from top to Groundscape and includes cutout, covered with amber light-gel, of large star and lines of "lead" connected by colored light-gel. There is an open space in the center of the Window into which the Holy Family puppet fits.
- Holy Family—Mary seated on bail of hay with Babe in her lap and Joseph standing beside her is one puppet. Mary's pregnant belly is a separate puppet held in place, covering the infant, until the birth.
- Cluster of Stars (representing Angel)

Stars are one puppet which is a cutout of connected star shapes filled with amber gel. This puppet appears suddenly from back to screen, on cue, and remain in constant motion during Angel's musical announcement.

- Two Shepherds—shorter than Joseph, are one joined puppet, but each shepherd has one moving arm and optional jointed torso.
- Sheep—three are one puppet joined together. One additional sheep enters separately.
- Crook—solid one piece puppet.
- Sun—Outline of sphere filled with amber gel with rays, one ray will Velcro in place on upper left corner of screen.
- Tree—A half tree with branches that extend to center screen. It will slide on from the right and attach to the additional Velcro along the edge of the screen.
- Flowers—three as one puppet rise up from groundscape and attach in place to Velcro on back of groundscape.
- Owl—with moving wings and large eyes. It flies in from one side and lands on tree branch attaching with Velcro.

Puppeteers:

(I suggest four, two male and two female. They become the live characters in the final scene. They will need to have costume bits (coats, hats, hoodys) to slip into easily and their gift props to carry on stage at hand)

This play will also require a narrator and a stage manager.

The shadow puppet screen (see Tips for Making Shadow Screen and Shadow Puppets section) is preset center stage/chancel with narrator's high stool and podium stage left and a bench and low stool stage right. House lights dim and back of screen spotlights come up revealing "stained glass window" with pregnant Mary and Joseph. All are held by puppeteers behind the screen. (Moment of silence)

The Shepherds

Scene One

Narrator:
Our drama begins in and around Bethlehem, a small village situated about 6 miles south of Jerusalem. This hamlet lies perched on a long, limestone ridge, enclosed from the north and the south by deep valleys. Here it was that the great King David was born. And here it was that he was anointed king of all Israel. The name Bethlehem, translated, means "the house of bread." The village was also known as "Ephrata" which means "the fertile."

We begin our tale with an event which happened approximately 2000 years ago, we don't know what day, month or even year, but we do know that this event took place when Israel was no longer a mighty realm but merely a province in the great Roman Empire and Augustus was ruler of that Empire. Augustus ordered a census be taken of all his citizens. and so, by law, as descendants of King David, Mary and Joseph traveled to their ancestral home of Bethlehem to be counted even though Mary was soon to give birth to her first child—a child who would grow to be known as the Christ or king of all humankind.

And in a humble shepherd's cave, under a star of remarkable brilliance, the child was born. (Puppets move for the first time as pregnancy turns into Baby—move pregnant belly puppet straight back to reveal Baby in Mary's lap)

Music: *Silent Night* (#119 *Common Praise*, Anglican hymnal)

(Toward the end of the music the "window" including M/J/B puppet disappears leaving the ground-scape only. This transition must be choreographed so as to be done as smoothly as possible) (When music ends shepherd and sheep puppets enter).

Scene Two

Narrator:
Scripture tells us that God sent an angel to herald this birth and chose shepherds in the fields near-by to be the first to receive the news—shepherds rather than the respectable, well bred, and powerful people of the day. Devout Jews held shepherds in utter contempt as shepherds were a half-savage people without roots and without home. Their nomadic existence did not permit them to attend services at the temple or a synagogue. Cleanliness was not one of their virtues as water was scarce on the plains where they lived. They were entirely ignorant of the Jewish prescriptions regulating daily life—the washing of hands and utensils, the choice of foods. What's more they were thieves and so it was unwise to buy wool or milk from them as these may well be stolen goods. (During this narration the shepherds scratch themselves, jostle each other and stroke their sheep).

Music (Angel's announcement—*While Shepherds Watched Their Flocks* #136 *Common Praise*, Anglican hymnal)

(Angel represented by "twinkling" multi-star puppet enters on screen. Shepards hold still pointing up to Angel. Moving the Angel puppet back from and forward to screen repeatedly will make stars disappear and reappear causing them to "twinkle").

Narrator:
The Shepherds no doubt well understood the words of the Angel. They had not the vast learning of the Pharisees, but as simple Jews they knew that one day the Messiah promised by the prophets would come. In the years of days and nights on these monotonous desert plains they perhaps often talked and dreamed of the great king who would one day come to Israel. (During this narration Shepherds gesture and interact)

Narrator:

The Shepherds made haste with joy. The fields about Bethlehem were, to them, familiar territory. They were going to visit a king, it is true, but this king dwelt in one of the caves that they knew so well.

[During this narration Shepherds and Sheep exit]

Music: *Joy To The World, Common Praise* #154

(During music Mary / Joseph / Babe puppet returns without Window. Shepherds and Sheep enter and move into place next to M/J/B puppet)

Scene Three

Narrator:

This is the ancient Christian story of an incarnational event—of God coming to Earth as a baby to dwell among us. And Christians have been responding to this event ever since.

(At end of narration Shepherds and Sheep exit—final sheep goes back for last look at Baby and is pulled off with crook by unseen hand)

Scene Four

Narrator:

Now, in the twenty-first century, where might we find this living event in our lives and in the world?

Music: *New Day Dawning* (see Music Resources)

(During music the M/J/B puppet disappears leaving the groundscape—the sun appears—the half-tree slowly appears sliding in from the side of the screen showing half a trunk and branches reaching out to center screen—the owl puppet flies in and settles in the tree's branches—flowers pop into view from the ground scape. (Each of these puppets is pressed into place with Velcro). Finally, the puppeteers enter from behind the screen. Two of them are shabbily dressed and two are smartly dressed in warm coats. One shabbily dressed person is carrying an infant, or if not possible, a life-like doll. They all move to stage right and arrange themselves on the preset bench and stool. Ideally this group should represent different races and ages. They sit companionably admiring the baby in the shabby man's arms.

As the stage right spotlight dims up on them, they present the new "holy family" with practical unwrapped gifts such as blanket, food, diapers, piggy bank.

Narrator:
Let us pray,
Creator God, thank you for the presence of Christ throughout history and in our lives today. The innumerable rebirths we experience in your beautiful world give us hope for peace, wisdom and love. Help us to honor and protect all life, to learn from our shadows and grow into the light as we celebrate Christmas every day.
Through Christ our Lord. Amen
(The four characters remain in tableau for a few beats then all exit together.) Reprise: *New Day Dawning*)

CHAPTER 10

Fire and Passion

ERNEST AND I ONCE spent a delightful month long holiday in Portugal. We rented a farmhouse in the tiny northern village of Sa and during our stay, Sa celebrated her annual saint's day. Apparently, every village in Portugal has a saint's day to joyfully mark the village's past, present and future. I don't know about the other villages but in Sa this is a three-day occasion. The twelve farm homes, two shops and chapel that make up the village are clustered together, like eggs in a nest, with their farmlands surrounding them. On the evening of their saint's day all twelve families—adults, children, dogs, babes in arms down their tools and join in a procession throughout the village. They gather at the chapel and walk full circle back to it along the hilly roads overlooking their homes where they have placed lit candles in all their windows. We joined the procession and the sight a top the hills was a valley of warm pinpoints of light nestled under the lush green and purple of grape vine canopies. Each walker also carried a candle with two men in front holding an effigy of St. Andrew aloft. In preparation for this annual liturgical event copious amounts of food is prepared and set out at the chapel along with everyone's musical instruments ready for the 72-hour celebration. Hopeful songs, prayers and toasts are offered to their saint and to God in thanksgiving for their health and harvests. To quote Meister Eckart, "If the only prayer you said was 'thank you' that would be enough."

These villagers experience their births, deaths and significant events together day by day, like one family. It was a privilege for us to share a piece of their celebratory liturgy with them. We reflected on the saints, past and present, in our own lives and communities and thought about what they mean to us.

As wayfarers passing through this village and unable to speak Portuguese our experience of the liturgy was incomplete. But it led us to think of the many other ritual, intensive liturgies available to us. Our interests and our personal and professional needs of the moment lead us to participate in some and not in others.

There are the pilgrimages for those who seek to mark a life change and can walk for months, silent retreats for those who thirst for deep meditation—sometimes for as long as forty days, a serious theatre production of dance, drama and/or music with its many weeks of single minded rehearsals as well as jazz, film and theatre festivals all of which have the potential to inspire us, re-creation events where masses of people live for a week or two in another era and in other's shoes and, of course, marathons of all kinds that support fire charities but exhaust me to think about!

Intensity and endurance woven with basic elements such as fire, water, and earth have always been at the core of change. One of the most written about and best-known biblical stories involves God's passion and hope for re-creation. It is our model for individual, less extreme, acts of renewal. God, discouraged by the evil in the world, chose one good man and his family along with a sampling of all living-kind to endure the ravages of a unique flood and survive, thus beginning Creation all over again. God makes a covenant with the good man, Noah, to never do this again and offers the rainbow as a sign of hope and a reminder of God's promise. At some level this story with its dramatic use of the element of water to wash away our corporate sins influences us as we reflect on our individual needs for renewal.

Often the ritual of fire is the element that intensifies our experiences of new beginnings—from the gentle warmth and comfort of a candle, a fireplace or a communal bonfire (our symbols of everlasting light) to the blazing torch we pass from one to another to represent our unity, to the burning and wearing of ashes on Ash Wednesday as we contemplate our mortality.

Today, in the western United States there is one intense celebration / life liturgy that fascinates me. It is known as Burning Man.

Life Liturgy, Outdoors, Communal Celebration

Burning Man is an annual event where a five- mile square temporary city, called Great Rock City, is built in the Nevada desert. Each year approximately fifty five thousand creative and artistic people make Great Rock City their home for one week.

It is an opportunity for people of all ages and backgrounds to experience renewal, self-discovery, and unrestricted self-expression. Here they can face fears and anxieties while having unreserved fun! Some go just to take in the atmosphere but most join small working groups to help build the city. The participants must come with or provide all food, water, shelter (tents, RVs) and materials for creating that they will need for the week. The planners with thirteen hundred volunteers take a full year to prepare so that others can create spontaneously.

Like any city the basics are put in place—fire department, police department, medical team, newsletter, large generator for power tools, and even an airport. There is a department of Public Works that carves out the roads and installs gas streetlights, which they light each night, and they build the Man. Each year the planners designate a different theme and the "Man" takes the shape of that theme. This forty-foot high "Man" dominates the city and it, along with attached altars, are ritually burned at the end of the event each year.

It is a life-changing experience that many people return to year after year. The ultimate live antidote for social media as most stay off the grid!

From the participants:

> "It's a remarkable experience to live in the town. The energy, freedom of expression and personal growth is mind blowing but when you keep coming to Burning Man you realize you have to be a part of the gift and it becomes a way of life."

Can God Come Out To Play?

I spoke with the daughter of a friend who attended Burning Man in the summer of 2013. For her, as I suspect for many, the outstanding aspect of the event was the art. Visual and performing artists are drawn to each other and to this desert setting with its vast space for building large-scale creations. Art-cars, made from bicycle parts, etc. are a popular mode of transportation. My informant said,

> "Great Rock City becomes one of the most impressive art galleries in the world.
>
> The artists can build anything they want but must provide all their own materials. Since the whole event is dedicated to working toward a better society, clean up at the end is essential. So, much of the art needs to be dismantled. Some artists take it home to reassemble and others are able to rent storage space in the near-by town so that they can continue working on their piece the following summer.
>
> Each participant registers to stay in a camp within the Great Rock City. The camps are made up of from 20 to 100 people in tents or RVs and each camp offers a gift to the whole community. These gifts would be anything that might appeal to a demographic of the whole such as: hair dressing salon, spa, sauna, bars, dance clubs, spirituality centers, supervised kids enclosures, reading and relaxation spots, specialty food vans, movie theatre, orgy tent—something for everyone!"

Great Rock is a noncommercial city. You must initially buy a ticket for yourself and pay a fee for your vehicle to cover the costs of the building materials for the city itself. These fees are kept as low as possible. There is nothing sold on site except coffee and ice.

The ideals of creative, noncommercial, cooperative living that are the foundation of Burning Man are spreading and now there are small "Burns" all over the world. One just opening in Israel.

My informant went on to say,

> "In theory there is total freedom to do what you wish, within the law, but there are some established practices that are somewhat dogmatic and could make those who

didn't want to participate in them feel uncomfortable—such as wearing costumes or wearing nothing at all."

Apparently the prevalence of nudity and drugs (not necessarily together) is common. It could be socially uncomfortable to go alone to this event; most travel there in a group which can then join the same camp.

At the end of the week there is the Burning Man Ceremony and for many this is a spiritual experience; for others a party. Some get married or remarried at Burning Man.

I'm told that the burning itself is the only occasion that all residents of Great Rock City are together at one time. It is also the only time that people are quiet. The liturgy becomes the focus with music, prayers and other spoken words, sometimes performances, and, of course, the burning of the Man. The city's small temples, on either side of the Man are also burned. The closing ceremony marks an incarnation or new beginning—a fresh start for many. Thousands write down past tragedies, regrets, broken resolves and sad events, such as the suicide of a friend, and place these written slips in the large temple bowls to include in the burning as an act of repentance or a symbol of transformation.

There have been numerous DVDs made of Burning Man. But *Journey To The Flames* is a one and a half hour documentary which is a montage of the events of eleven years (1998—2007 and 2010) It is available through many public library systems.

Chapter 11

What's In A Name?

Here is an Angolan folktale.

A young man had four brothers. He met a girl and married her. The bride slept the four days of brideship. Then she went out of the house and set a pot of gruel on the fire. She cooked the gruel until it was done. She took out a plateful for her husband, and four platefuls for her brothers-in-law. She went to bring the food to them.

Her brothers-in-law said to her,
"If we eat this gruel, tell us our names." She said,
"I do not know your names." They said,
"If you do not know our names, take away the gruel."
She took it up and went with it to her house. The husband and wife ate the gruel.

The same thing happened the next day. The woman was thinking to herself, "My brothers-in-law refuse to eat my gruel. But I do not know their names."

The next day, at sundown, the woman took cassava roots to pound them into flour. She went to the mortar, put the tubers into it, and began to pound them with a pestle.

A little bird flew down to the tree near the mortar. It began to sing:

What's In A Name?

"Your brothers-in-law,
You know not their names?
Listen; I shall tell you!"
She pounds the tubers!
"One is Tumba Sikundu
One is Tumba Sikundu Muna.
Listen; I shall tell you!
One is Tumba Kaulu,
One is Tumba Kaulu Muna.
Listen; I shall tell you!"
She pounds the roots!
"Listen; I have told you."

The young woman threw the pestle to the ground. She picked up a stone to chase away the bird. "It is making such noise," she said. The little bird flew away.

When the flour was ready she took it into the house and set a pot of gruel on the fire. When it was done she took platefuls to her brothers-in-law. They said to her, "Tell us our names." She said,

"I do not know your names."

They said, "Take away the gruel."

She took it back and went into her house. She and her husband ate the gruel.

The next day she returned to the mortar to pound cassava tubers again. As she began, the same little bird came to tell her once more what it had tried to share with her the previous day. She chased it away again. But after it was gone, she realized what the little bird was telling her. "It was telling me the names of my brothers-in-law. Now I understand."

When the flour was ready, she took it to her house and put a pot of gruel on the fire. When it was done, she took platefuls of gruel to her brothers-in-law. They said to her, "If we eat your gruel, tell us our names."

The woman said, "This one is Tumba Sikundu; this one, Tumba Sikundu Muna; this one, Tumba Kaulu; this one, Tumba Kaulu Muna."

Her brothers in-law laughed. They accepted the gruel and ate it.

We identify so closely with our names. They connect us with family, culture, history, and self-image. Liking or disliking our names is akin to liking or disliking ourselves. We all know people who, when reaching an age of maturity, rename themselves. Sometimes they take their middle name or a name that is etymologically close to theirs, Sarah rather than Sally or Alexandra rather than Sandra, remaining loyal to their birth names while adjusting their name to better suit their self-image. Some claim a name that is entirely different from the one they have grown up with. Others welcome a nickname given to them by friends as a gesture of familiarity and, some change their family names in marriage. Then there are those who don't change their names at all!

But what ever we do or don't do with our names they remain a vital part of our personal history and family identity. "I don't care what you print about me, just make sure you spell my name right!" Our names are tied to our self-identities and therefore to our self-esteem. Forgetting a person's name or getting it wrong can be hurtful to that person and embarrassing to the one in error.

All this builds a stressful pressure around names, "I always remember a face but I have such difficulty remembering names." It might be illuminating to make a list of the individual names we can't remember and ask ourselves, "Why?" There are books that teach specific techniques for remembering names, but I suspect there are some names we simply block out. I can think of politicians whose names are mentioned daily in the news but for some reason when called upon to refer to them I can't remember their names!

Our names are also emblematic of our culture and as a result naming has theological, social and political implications. In the Judeo/Christian tradition God gave Adam the task of naming all creatures and all things. And we know who the important characters in the Bible are because they are named. This is particularly significant if they are women as most women in the Bible are not named at all. In the Christian Bible Christ is given some 200 names or titles, presumably to show that only one name would not be sufficient to glorify him.

What's In A Name?

In the Christian sacrament of Baptism the parents are asked, "Name this child" and baptism is the entry rite to the community. In fact, the unbaptised are excluded from the invitation to receive communion in many Christian religions. I can't help seeing this practice as inhospitable.

In Christianity Man has the God-given right to be the name-giver. But Jesus was not so interested in the business of names, not even his own. He said at one point, "Not everyone who calls me Lord, Lord will enter the Kingdom of Heaven but only those who do the will of my heavenly Father," (Matt. 7:21).

Everybody and every thing has a name and is distinguishable by it. Name-giving is accompanied by a formidable power which has often been abused. It should be remembered, however, that the original name-giver(s), Adam for one, gave names to the unnamed as opposed to our coercing those from other countries to change their names.

I quote C.S. Song from his book, *Tell Us Our Names: Story Theology From an Asian Perspective*,

> "At the root of Christian faith, there is a strong consciousness of the power to name things, the power to keep the objects named under control. In modern times scientists and technologists in the West, strongly influenced by the Christian ethos, fully exploited this name giving power. They set about exploring the universe, conquering it, naming it, and putting it under their control. This is how our scientific and technological civilization was born. Ours is a civilization built on our naming-power over the objective world."

Like scientists we Christians have tended to misuse the name-giving power in relation to persons outside the church. Intentionally or not, we forget that this particular power is the power that shapes, changes, and controls those who have come into contact with it. Song continued,

> "... Africa and Asia were not "christianized," but missionaries and Christian converts joined forces to 'christen' persons they had won and territories they had

> conquered. Great power was released in this 'christening' mission—the power to change others and to estrange them from their cultural roots.
>
> A name is not just the name of an individual. It is the name of the family, of the tribe, of a people. In that name lives a history and in that name past, present, and future converge. That is why names have a particular meaning in Asia and Africa. Name giving is not so much exercise in power as performance of family duty."

And, of course, we think not only of Asia and Africa but also our North American Native Peoples.

Perhaps it is not name-giving power that is needed but name-knowing power. If we listen to the little bird we may gain the wisdom to identify names, to pronounce them correctly, and to understand and experience their deep meanings.

Liturgies of Naming

There are a wide variety of customs of naming in the different faiths, and cultures around the world. The diversity of naming-rituals includes the use of elements such as fire, smoke, water, tree planting and honey! The importance of family, past and present, and the chanting or reading of a sacred text are common features in a name-giving ceremony.

In many cases timing of the ceremony is significant—the time elapsed after birth or a relationship of the name to the configuration of the stars at the time of birth. Apparently, in all traditions the naming of a new life is a vitally important symbol of a fresh start.

Some naming traditions have follow-up rituals. There is a Jewish tradition of planting a tree at the birth of a child (cedar for a boy, pine for a girl) and when the baby has grown and marries the tree is cut down and made into the poles of the wedding tent.

Native American naming traditions may have the greatest variety of all as they vary significantly from tribe to tribe. Their naming traditions are frequently determined by nature, animals, or their characters.

The Miwok tribe has a custom of using water names, often chosen by the way the stream flowed when a baby was born.

The Southwest Hopis have a mystic tradition of placing an ear of corn, representing Mother Earth, close to a newborn baby. Twenty days after the birth, corn is rubbed over the baby's body while the baby, held to face the rising sun, is named when the first ray of sun hits his/her forehead.

The Navajos give great powers to their names. A Navajo name is deemed so precious that it is only used during ceremonies. Therefore a day-to-day conversation in a Navajo family may go something like, "Mother, go get Son."

The Salish tribe follows a "naming trail" in which the name given to a baby by the parents at birth (usually a virtue or trait the parents hope for in the baby) is eventually replaced during adolescence with another name which is given by the tribal leader at a ceremony called the Jump Dances. This name normally signifies a gift or strength for which the child is known. Similarly, as an adult, another name might be granted, but this name would reflect expectations for the person to live up to.

Traditionally without family names, the Sioux (Lakota, Nakota and Dakota) have a complicated naming system with six classes of names: birth order, honor, special deed, nicknames, secret and spirit names. The first name is given based on the gender and birth position of the child, and a person could have several names during his/her lifetime depending on personal characteristics.

It is common practice today to use kinship terms, such as Uncle or Grandfather, for people who are not related to show respect.

This is just a sampling of naming ceremonies to show the breadth and importance of naming traditions around the world.

Here, from the Christian tradition is a hymn and a biblical reference to look at naming from a musical and poetic perspective.

Genesis 32: 22–32

Song from *More Voices* #161 *I Have Called You By Your Name.*

Chapter 12

Creative Juices

GOD IS NOT CREATIVE—GOD is creativity itself—God is the world's first known entrepreneur!

Many have the potential entrepreneur inside them but some have to learn how to stretch the imagination to access it.

There was a time, not long ago, when people worked for a single employer all their lives. However, the days of secure jobs from school graduation to the gold watch are over. Now, many feel forced into entrepreneurship in order to make a living, while some cannot imagine any other lifestyle. Artists, for instance, have always thrived, while starving, on the heady independence of being their own bosses. But artists are not the only ones who can enjoy the freedom of designing the choreography and brush strokes of their careers.

In fact, increasingly, entrepreneurship is becoming the norm in the twenty-first century. It requires lateral thinking and surely this kind of creative survival thinking has been around since the dawn of time.

"Look! If I drag this rock against this other rock long enough it becomes a pointy thing!"

"Junior, stop rubbing those two sticks together. Remember what happened the last time!"

And, Archangel to God: "God, Your people have become waaay too wicked. Do you think its time for plan B? I'll get the umbrellas."

And so forth throughout the ages.

But since formal education began we have been trained to think in a linear or vertical way which relies solely on logic. Lateral thinking requires us to use creative imagination where instead of trying the same thing over and over to reach our goal we take a step sideways and look at the situation from another angle. A simple example:

My son, who is a very tall man, found that his queen-sized bed was not long enough for comfort. He designed, in his head, various small benches on which he could put a mattress-thick six inch length of foam to attach to the foot of the bed for lengthening it. Then lateral (horizontal?) thinking kicked in and he realized that the piece of foam could be put at the head of the bed wedged between the headboard and the mattress and, with no carpentry, the bed was six inches longer!

Lateral thinking is not giving up. A "new" concept, invention or solution is just a fresh way of assembling "old" parts. Lateral or creative thinking requires us to seize opportunities which initially seem either risky or frivolous but then appear to be an obvious choice in hindsight.

Edward de Bono is credited with the name and concept of lateral thinking—thinking outside the box, etc. He has written many books on the subject including school curricula and his *de Bono Group* regularly gives workshops in lateral thinking. It is a valuable tool, but not just for getting ahead in the world. Lateral / creative thinking can help us discover ourselves as the unique human beings we are and to side-step the actions that for no other reason "have always been done this way." Learning to let go of old habits and rituals to broaden our perspectives and create new rituals is how we grow and mature especially if in the doing we come to better accept our own uniqueness.

Actors often learn creative thinking through theatre games, based on improvisation which has three rules:

1. Take the first thought that comes to you. In improvisation it is always the best even if it is a risk.
2. No creative blocking. When another player establishes a who, what, or where it is fact for the scene. You can love or hate that fact but you can't negate it.
3. Accept the offer—meaning say yes to another's idea and build on it. If one player says the rug is on fire and the other immediately produces a fire extinguisher this will not be creative blocking but it will not be accepting the offer either. It would be better to react to the fire and build on that offer to the scene. In improvisational drama don't try to solve problems; accept them as gifts for the scene.

These rules are as useful for us in daily life as they are for actors in developing positive, creative thought. So with these rules in mind try the following exercises, alone or with others, to begin releasing your creative imagination.

Point and Name

You and any others who wish to join you walk around a reasonably furnished space pointing at random objects calling each item by the first word that comes to your mind rather than by its actual name. This can be done for one minute, out loud, and simultaneously with the others. It is meant to help you release and use your first thoughts.

Yes But, Yes And

To be done in pairs.
One person begins a positive, enthusiastic sentence such as " I love the first clean white snow of winter." The other replies, "Yes but" and continues with a negative remark like, " It soon turns black and ugly and all we have left is the cold." Each person can then pause and reflect on how it felt to have her positive remark put down and how it felt to be the one who gave the put-down.

Then reverse roles with one person again making a positive remark but this time the second person begins his sentence with, "Yes and" and then builds on the other's positive statement. This is an exercise in accepting the offer.

A Life Liturgy

Here is a true story I wrote about a seized opportunity in my life. It recalls a personal event that helped me learn that win or lose it's playing the game creatively that matters. Whether or not you solve your problems, attacking them creatively will provide positive and memorable experiences.

My prayer for all of you, dear readers, is that you follow your creative imaginations wherever they lead you despite risks, doubts and other's objections. When you go out to play, sometimes it seems doors will close, plans fall through, and games end, but if you take a positive sideways-step-view of your situation you won't be disappointed. And you may gain a life-liturgy to remember.

Between Engagements written by Sally Armour Wotton

An actor is never out of work—just between engagements

I was twenty-five, stuck in California, out of work, and out of money—staying with my friends, Norman and Pete. They had a suburban house and life style in Los Angeles and thought my theatre experiences were exotic, giving them stories to tell their office colleagues.

Their TV was a handy surface on which to set my peanut butter sandwich and *Let's Make A Deal* was just coming on. I'd caught snatches of this quiz show before. It was perfect. It required absolutely no skill or knowledge from its contestants. There were no tests or auditions; I only needed some idiotic prop or costume to take with me to trade for a prize. The show didn't give out money but at least it had the potential of awarding something saleable. Monty, the host, strode onto the set and applause erupted. I flicked the volume down thinking, "What an awful job that must be; still, he has the gleaming white teeth and the pompadour hair, not to mention the obvious shoulder pads in his suit, so I guess he's destined for it."

Can God Come Out To Play?

I thought of myself, at the time, as a serious actress, one who didn't happen to have a job at the moment. Actually, I hadn't had a job for the last two months of moments. I'd hoped that the touring show that brought me from New York to Los Angeles and promptly closed would reopen, but that looked less likely every day. I had friends, contacts and opportunities in New York but no money to get back there.

Norm and Pete had put me up in their home for nearly a month and now Pete's Mum was coming to visit them. It was time for me to move out of their guest room. I didn't even have enough money left to pay for the peanut butter I was eating. So, a game show was my obvious next step!

Let's Make A Deal would be taping at the end of the week and would choose the contestants from the throng waiting outside the studio. "I need a prop," I thought, "something to trade. Which of my host's ugly lamps will they miss the least? No, there'll be a million lamps, I need something that will stand out."

It was Norman who gave me the idea. He came home from the launderette that evening and said,

"Look what I've got — cleaning rags for the next ten years! This sheet got caught on the spin thingy and ripped right down the middle." Pete answered,

"And you brought it home? Like we need cleaning rags? Into the garbage!"

Norm and Pete were good people but imagination-challenged. There were, of course, a million things you could do with a torn sheet. With sudden inspiration I grabbed this particular torn sheet, got some felt markers and a wire coat hanger, and enlisted the help of the others to fashion a giant envelope complete with drawn on stamp and flap and a straightened coat hanger across my shoulders to square it off. We addressed it to the television studio and when the pins were in place it fit me perfectly. The studio moguls couldn't refuse such an imposing letter addressed to them, could they?

Norm and Pete drove me to the television studio in Burbank and left me there. Left me with six hundred others (the count was announced on a loud speaker). They were all standing in the studio parking lot with their elephant-foot ashtrays and their deformed garden gnomes. I looked around, taking in my competition. There was an old car seat that glowed in the dark, a full-sized paper machete replica of Donald Duck, a rainbow-painted toilet bowl on wheels, the widest range of drop-dead designer lamps ever gathered in one place, and one man dressed as a Scottish highlander apparently prepared to trade his bagpipes. I was in good company. We were marshaled into long lines, about fifteen hopeful dealers deep as four men walked slowly in front of us occasionally choosing a contestant.

I stepped into line next to some small native Los Angeleans with elbows they had sharpened for the occasion. Luckily, I had an advantage. At 6' 2," with coat hanger enhanced shoulders, I was still quite noticeable even when prodded to the rear. I saw one of the men responsible for the choosing straining to read my envelope. I shouldered my way forward and the man said,

"Hey, that's good. OK, you're number 36. Here's your ticket."

I, in my envelope, was now one of the forty who would sit on the prize floor section of the studio audience. Of course, there's only time for about six people to "make a deal" in the half hour allotted, so another hurdle remained.

I was given an aisle seat and my good fortune persisted as Monty, now full size and more intimidating than he was on a 21-inch screen, approached me. "What's this?" he said, eyeing the enormous envelope sitting upright in the chair. I held my breath trying not to notice his shock of hair that appeared to have a life of its own perched above those glittering teeth. A glance at Monty's eyes told me he was somewhere far from this studio, but had put himself on automatic pilot set at high enthusiasm. He looked electrically wired as he said,

"Is this a letter addressed to us?"

The envelope and I regained our composure. We nodded yes as we rose to our full height. He responded with,

"My, this must have cost a fortune in postage."

The studio audience laughed on cue. His voice rose in pitch and volume as he asked,

"Now, would you be willing to trade this envelope for that mysterious, wrapped gift on the table?"

I found myself matching his energy level.

"Yes! I'll trade!!"

The studio audience was electronically prompted to outdo us both, and a kind of frenzy took over. There was a drum roll, and the gift was unwrapped. It was a set of encyclopedias.

I tried to maintain a show of enthusiasm as I thought, "Who in heaven's name will buy that? And in any case how would the sale provide enough to get me back to New York?"

However, it had been an experience. I was still poor, but now I thought, "I will be knowledgeable and poor."

I began to relax into a spectator role, but I had never watched the end of this show. Therefore, it came as a surprise to me when Monty said,

"Now . . . which two of tonight's charming contestants shall I choose to try for the grand prize?"

I thought, "This guy is a very powerful man." I shifted back into frenzied contestant mode and tried to catch his eye. He toyed with us,

"Which of you brilliant six folks could bear to trade your first prize for what is behind one of those three doors?"

I glanced around at my now extremely alert companions and then as I trained an intense gaze on our host I heard him say,

"Will the gentleman who brought the stuffed bird of unknown species and the lady who arrived by special delivery post please come forward?"

On the signal from the electric sign, the audience broke into wildly excited applause. The stuffed birdman and I made an amusing pair—he at about 5'8" trying to appear cool with a large, multicolored, obviously dead, bird under his arm and I, towering over him, in my now crumpled envelope with the thoroughly smudged zip code. We waited in suspended time to point at our chosen door as the prospective prizes were described.

Behind one of the doors there was a living room suite of furniture. I thought, "Heaven forbid—that would be next to impossible to sell even in the unlikely event that it was attractive." Behind another door there was a full-size plaster cow. In my crazed state of mind I considered, "If it's mechanized, I may get back to New York City yet." The remaining door had five sets of brand name towels. "Bingo. Those will probably sell and if not, at least, I can live with them."

My bird fancier colleague was summoned to join Monty in the spotlight. His arm floated up into a pointing position as the studio music rose toward a crescendo. Unsteadily and in slow motion his finger wavered between door number one and door number three. Then his arm moving like a bicycle on a gravel road aimed itself at door number one and locked in.

Door number one slid back and revealed the suite of furniture, which was more hideous than my worst imaginings. He was thrilled. The audience was ecstatic.

Monty gestured for me to join him. He took a dramatic pause and said,

"What would you do with old plaster Bessie if it happens that you choose her as a prize? She'd make a stunning addition to any front garden especially accompanied by pink flamingos."

I mumbled something inane, which was mercifully masked by the audience's laughter at our host's wit. As the laughter died down my arm began to twitch in anticipation of its task. It rose to pointing position and aimed itself squarely and decisively at door three. I couldn't have moved it if I had wanted to. The door began to slide open and I thought I heard a soft mechanized moo.

But no. There were the thick brightly colored towels—reds, yellows and oranges displayed like a glorious sunset. It was my turn to be thrilled but just as my relief and excitement reached its peak the towels magically moved away to unveil a state of the art, color coordinated washer and dryer.

"Alleluia!" I nearly shouted aloud. "Utilities will sell!"

After-word

WE HAVE PLAYED WITH God since the beginning of time—through the archaic dance of sacred mythology, during a thousand years of paradise on Earth, followed by centuries of passionate politics, into the devout centuries of medieval preparation for life after death, through the last hundred years co creating with and finding God within, and at this time of questions and doubts. It seems the majority of people now, in the West at least, either embrace the unquestioning Fundamentalism or doubt there is a God at all. As I am part of the questioning humanity of today, I see the possibility of a nonexistent God.

However, at the same time I know there is so much I don't know. Therefore, I choose to return to the Archaics but with twenty first century sensibilities and believe in the Mystery. An all-powerful Mystery, that is in us and beyond us, is to me the most logical conclusion to the God question. The remarkable and continual discoveries of the unknown, tucked hidden beneath the known, through science, philosophy and the arts regularly affirm my belief in the Mystery.

Every time we take ourselves too seriously and think we have all the answers our mysterious God finds a way to remind us that our value and importance lays in our insignificance—that each of us is a miniscule but irreplaceable piece of a puzzle too enormous for us to perceive. The Yiddish proverb says it well, "Man plans; God laughs."

But perhaps this brief quote from the full-length one-woman play, *The Search For Signs of Intelligent Life in the Universe* by Jane Wagner best encapsulates the themes from this book.

> Trudy: "My space chums and I are thinking, maybe the secrets about life we don't understand are the 'cosmic' carrots in front of our noses that keep us going. So maybe we should stop trying to figure out the meaning of life and sit back and enjoy the mystery of life.
>
> Well, next my chums insisted I take them somewhere they could get goose bumps; they were dying to see what it was like. So I decided we'd take in a play, I got goose bumps once that way. On the way to the theatre we stopped to look at the stars and as usual I felt in awe. And then I felt even deeper in awe at this capacity we have to feel in awe about something. Then I became even more awe struck about the fact that I was in some small way a part of that which I was in awe about. And this feeling went on and on and on. My space chums have a word for it—awe infinitum. Because at the point you can comprehend just how incomprehensible it all is you're about as smart as you ever need to be. And at the moment you are most in awe of all that you don't understand you are closer to understanding it all than at any other time."

Let us grow forth through our shadows into our divinity-within with laughter and playfulness.

Thanks be to God.

Tips for Making Shadow Screen and Shadow Puppets

Overview

Shadow puppets are an ancient form of puppetry, originating in the Far East. They are two-dimensional; the early ones made of goat-skin (first chewed then dried). They are operated by puppeteers pressing them with handles or rods against the back of a cloth screen that is stretched taut on a frame. The lights must be off in front of the screen where the audience is seated. A strong light, behind the screen and above the heads of the puppeteers, is focused on the puppets. Thus the audience sees the "shadow" of the puppets.

The puppets are jointed and moved by attached sticks / rods, or handles. Detail, such as eyes and costume design is provided by cutting holes in the puppet to let the light come through. Features or embellishments cannot be drawn on the puppet as drawings would simply dissolve into the black shape or shadow. Intricate costume details can be formed with pinpricks and color is produced by covering the holes with theatre light gel.

TIPS FOR MAKING SHADOW SCREEN AND SHADOW PUPPETS

Traditional puppets from Indonesia and Bangkok

Shadow puppets are normally designed and cut in profile so that they can interact with one another on a flat screen.

Well made and sensitively operated shadow puppets have an intrinsic dignity and beauty and are effective when mimed to music and narration rather than performed with character voices.

To be seen the puppets must remain pressed against the back of the screen. They can enter or exit by sliding on or off the sides of the screen, but for a dramatic exit the puppeteer, holding the puppet, can take a step backward to move the puppet out of the light and therefore make it instantly disappear.

This Play:

The intention is to tell the Nativity story through shadow puppets, music and the attached script which is narrated. The Holy Family puppet is designed to form the center piece of a "stained glass window." This would be the visual for the opening of the performance and as the narration unfolds the puppet begins to move in the window tableau and come to life.

Tips for Making Shadow Screen and Shadow Puppets

Shadow Screen:

The shadow screen begins as a simple wooden frame much like a picture frame. It can be any size. I have one that is two feet by five feet of 1" x 2" lumber and I also have one that is eight feet by fourteen feet of 2" x 4" lumber. The size depends on how large you need the production to be based on the size of the venue and audience. The puppets are made in profile so usually move from side to side. For that reason and for stability the puppet screen should be approximately twice as wide as it is high.

When you have built your frame you will need to cover the back/puppeteer side of it with white fabric such as sheeting. When in place this covering must be very taut. So, to attach the cloth, first staple continuing strips of Velcro along all four sides of the frame. Cut the cloth to fit the frame tightly when hemmed then sew the accompanying Velcro along all four sides of the cloth. Stretch and press the cloth, Velcro to Velcro, onto the frame. This will make a firm, tight surface for the puppets to press against and be seen and it allows the white fabric to be easily removed and washed from time to time and to be stored. If you are making a large screen, I suggest using bolts and wing nuts instead of screws in your construction. This permits easy disassembly for travel or storage.

Set Up:

The screen will need to stand up off the floor for visibility of puppets and ease of manipulation. I suggest using a long table, such as a folding style banquet table. Cover the table with a cloth to the floor in the front for a finished look and to mask the puppeteer's legs. Screw a length of 1" x 4" lumber to the full length of the bottom of the frame and attach this to the back edge of the table with C clamps. A very large screen will need additional support such as two braces made of 1" x 2" lumber—each attached to the back of the screen frame near the top corners and angling out down to the floor like an easel. Sandbags or other heavy weights should be attached to the bottom of these brace-supports for stability.

Tips for Making Shadow Screen and Shadow Puppets

To Mask Entrances and Exits:

If the shadow puppet set up is on a traditional stage, simply draw the stage curtains in to meet it. If not on a stage, you can put a tall folding screen on either side of the set up or cut two short pieces of 1" x 2" lumber for arms to extend outward from either side of the top of the frame. Drill a hole through one end of each arm and drill the same size hole just in from the top corner of each end of the screen frame through which you can attach the arms to the screen with a bolt and wing nut. Staple a panel of dense fabric, that extends to the floor, to each of the arms to form side-masking extensions.

Puppet Materials:

Before you begin to chew your goatskin, I recommend that you visit an arts supply store and buy a sheet or two of black Coroplast (a corrugated plastic sheeting) as your basic material, some Chicago Screws to attach moving parts, and a mat knife. You will also need theatre light gel in bright colors, small diameter Dowling, and a piece of chalk and some newsprint for making patterns. If theatre light gel is unavailable, colored tissue paper, though less robust, will do. In addition to the above you will need scissors, duct tape, small plastic self-stick kitchen or bathroom hooks, and a small hacksaw. For creating puppet eyes and costume details it will be useful to have a single-hole punch, an awl, and a large needle or nail.

Puppet Construction:

- Groundscape -
  A solid groundscape, slightly hilly, cut from Coroplast, along which the puppets move is attached to and across the length of the bottom of the screen and remains there throughout the play.

- Stained Glass Window—should cover most of the screen except for several inches at the bottom of the screen for the groundscape.

    Lay a large sheet of Coroplast on a worktable. From the center of this sheet cut out the single puppet of Mary/Joseph/Baby, with your mat knife, and then cut out random shapes all around this opening to create "stained glass." Leave a 2" border around the shapes to represent the lead of a stained glass window. One shape should be a large star at the top. Cover all your cut out openings, except the M/J/B opening, with colored gel or tissue paper and duct tape the gel in place. You may wish to draw your openings and "Lead" lines on the Coroplast first, with chalk, before cutting.

    It would be wise to experiment with the designs of the puppets on newsprint until you get the look and the scale that you want before cutting the Coroplast. The Internet has many sites with shadow puppet templates that are worth looking at for a clearer concept of this art form. I also recommend the small but helpful book, *Making Shadow Puppets*, Search Press, 1971—still in print at this writing.

- Holy Family—This puppet is what you have cut from the center of the "window." Mary seated on bail of hay with Babe in her lap and Joseph standing beside her. All together this is one puppet. Mary's pregnant belly is a separate puppet made from one of the discarded shapes of Coroplast. Cut it to just cover the Baby in Mary's lap. It will be held in place, covering the infant, until the birth. With your hole-making tools create eyes and costume details and cut random openings in costumes to cover with color.

- Cluster of Stars (representing Angel) -

    Stars are one puppet. Cut out the outline of star shapes that overlap securely to make a single puppet. Cover their open centers with amber gel. They appear suddenly from back to screen, on cue, and remain in constant motion.

- Two Shepherds—shorter than Joseph, are one overlapping puppet. They are in profile and each has a moving arm and optional jointed torso for bowing. As before, I suggest you experiment with newsprint to make a pattern. You will need to cut off their pattern arms and redraw extended arms so that there is an overlap on the shoulders to receive a joint. On the finished puppet, punch a hole through this extension on the arm and the shoulder and put in a Chicago Screw for the joint. If you feel ambitious you can do the same thing at their waists to allow them to bow or do this lower down for kneeling. I suggest both Shepherds and Joseph and Mary be designed with long gowns to avoid legs. This will make them more solid, less apt to break and easier to move.

Coroplast puppet with moving arm.

Tips for Making Shadow Screen and Shadow Puppets

- Three Sheep—are one puppet overlapping each other at the shoulders. One additional sheep enters separately.
- Shepherd's Crook—solid one piece puppet.
- Sun—outline of sphere filled with amber gel with rays, one ray will Velcro in place on upper left corner of screen.
- Tree—a half tree with branches. It will slide on from the right and attach to Velcro running along edge of screen frame.
- Flowers—three as one puppet rises up from groundscape and attaches in place to Velcro on back of groundscape.
- Owl—with moving wings, flies in from side and lands on tree branch and attaches with Velcro. Puppeteer can put two fingers in owl's eyeholes moving the fingers so that the puppet looks from side to side.

Operating Puppets:

After you have connected the moving part(s) to your puppets attach the movement rods.

For an up-right figure, duct tape a flat stick up the center of the entire back of the puppet extending several inches below the bottom to hold the puppet and press it against the screen.

If the arm is your moving part, attach the smallest diameter dowel to the back of the hand, by making a notch around and toward the end of the dowel and tying strong string, such as fish line, around the notch. Then thread the rest of string through the hand and tie it securely. Put a dot of white glue on the knots.

Puppets such as the pregnant belly, sheep, crook, stars, tree, sun and flowers can be held against the screen and moved with small plastic bathroom / kitchen self stick hooks which you attach to the back of the puppet and hold as handles. For the owl use the plastic hook on the back and a rod for the wings which should be one piece attached by a Chicago screw to the center of the puppet.

Tips for Making Shadow Screen and Shadow Puppets

Lighting:

Lighting is crucial for shadow puppets. When the performance is ready to begin all house lights are extinguished and the puppet lights come on. These lights should be spotlights clamped above the heads of the puppeteers (so that the puppeteers will not cast a shadow on the screen) and four to six feet behind the puppeteers. The lights must not be placed higher than the screen unless there is masking for them or they will shine in the eyes of the audience. If this production is not in a theatre, first make sure that the power load in your venue has the capacity to carry these extra lights.

You can rig the lights by setting up two stepladders four to six feet behind the screen with the distance of the width of the screen between them. C clamp a plank or 2"x 4" piece of lumber to the tops of the ladders, joining them. Then clamp the spotlights to the plank or 2x4 aiming them on the screen. Have enough spotlights so that the light is overlapped and the screen is completely and solidly lit. For maximum effect, attach a dimmer or dimmers to these lights so that they can all come on at once.

The ladders need to be taller than the puppeteers or the puppeteers will need to operate on their knees on cushions. For safety, weight the ladders so that during performance if they are bumped into they will not topple over. If there are cords hanging loose or on the floor thoroughly duct tape them to the surface so that no one trips or catches on them. Always have an extra lamp or two at hand in case one burns out.

Suggested Further Reading

Re-enchantment of Art, Suzi Gablik
The Myth of the Eternal Return, Mercia Eliade
Gaia: The Human Journey from Chaos to Cosmos, Elisabet Sahtouris
Sacred Folly-A New History of The Feast of Fools, Max Harris
The Feast of Fools—A Theological Essay on Festivity and Fantasy, Harvey Cox
The Stillness Without Shadows, Joseph J. Juknialis
The Dream of The Earth, Thomas Berry
The Great Work: Our Way Into The Future, Thomas Berry
Tell Us Our Names: Story Theology From an Asian Perspective, C.S. Song
The Search for Signs of Intelligent Life in the Universe, Jane Wagner (a full length one-woman play)
An Inconvenient Truth, Al Gore (also on DVD and CD)
Journey To The Flames, a documentary of Burning Man (DVD)
The Healing Oasis, Sharon Moon and Gary Sprague (CD)
Making Shadow Puppets, Search Press
Biblical quotes and references in this book are from the New Revised Standard Version, NRSV

Music Resources

CDs:

Songs Of Presence, Lynn C. Bauman, PRAXIS and All Saints Episcopal Church, Corpus Christi Texas, 2001
All My Life, Kelly Walker (selected songs, music and lyrics, included, with permission, in this book)
Spirit, Richard Stoltzman, RCA Victor 1995
Music of Unity and Peace, Taize Community
Day By Day, and *By My Side* from the musical, *Godspell,* Stephen Schwartz

Music books and hymnals:

Voices United, United Church Publishing House, Toronto, Ontario 1997
More Voices, United Church Publishing House, Toronto, Ontario and Woodlake Publishing Inc., Toronto, Ontario 2008
Taiza Community, Psalter Hymnal (Gray) 1982
Anglican Hymnal, *Common Praise,* Anglican Book Centre 1998

The following pages are songs recommended in these liturgies, not otherwise in print.

MUSIC RESOURCES
Songs by Kelly Walker Used in This Book's Liturgies

Hymn to Mother Earth

Kelly Walker

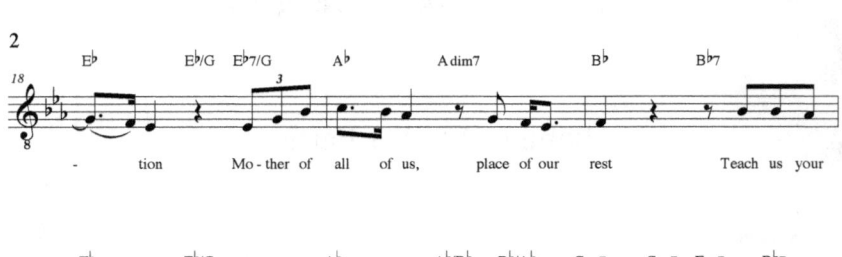
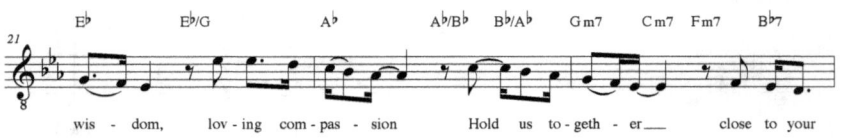
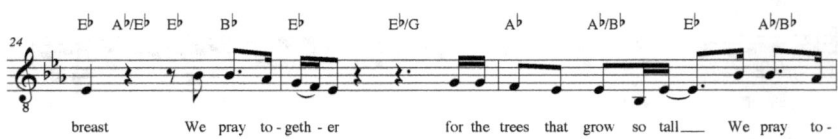
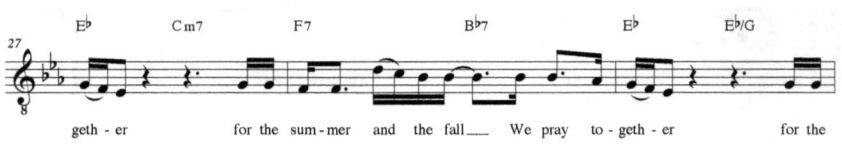

Paradise

Kelly Walker

Music Resources

Music Resources

MUSIC RESOURCES

Going Home

Kelly Walker

Music Resources

2

Music Resources

Music Resources

www.ingramcontent.com/pod-product-compliance
Lightning Source LLC
Chambersburg PA
CBHW070500090426
42735CB00012B/2629